Selena resides in Washington State with her husband and two dogs. She is a mother of two grown children whom she adores. When she isn't with her loved ones, she spends time reading, enjoying lattes, and planning escapes from the cold winters. She enjoys yoga, walks in the sun, a good workout in the mornings, and cozy evenings in. Listening to other people's stories is her inspiration for growth, as she believes all healing work begins in knowing we all have one to share.

To my love: You are home for me. We have been intertwined since the moment I met you and you know me from beginning to end. Your unending support has been everything. Your love without strings has been my saving grace.

To my sister: Here we are. We have been in this since day one and though our paths were unique to us, we made it. It has been a journey of winding roads to navigate and so many hills to climb. I am so proud of you.

To my children: My girls. My reason for everything. You have brought all good things to life for me. My inspiration to grow, to heal, to live fully, to not settle but to know a better way. To do everything possible within me to give you everything that was possible in you. I adore you.

To my darling friend: Wherever you are, I did it. I hope you know this book was written. You inspired me to write it all those years ago, encouraged me because you loved to read anything I wrote. I miss you every day. Thank you.

Selena Wade

POLLIWOG HUNTING

AUSTIN MACAULEY PUBLISHERS™

LONDON • CAMBRIDGE • NEW YORK • SHARJAH

Ordering Information
Quantity sales: Special discounts are available on quantity purchases by corporations, associations, and others. For details, contact the publisher at the address below.

Publisher's Cataloging-in-Publication data
Wade, Selena
Polliwog Hunting

ISBN 9798889103349 (Paperback)
ISBN 9798889103356 (ePub e-book)

Library of Congress Control Number: 2023918425

www.austinmacauley.com/us

First Published 2024
Austin Macauley Publishers LLC
40 Wall Street, 33rd Floor, Suite 3302
New York, NY 10005
USA

mail-usa@austinmacauley.com
+1 (646) 5125767

My dad: proud and stubborn, a perfectionist and loyal, honest and forthright. He is a myriad of good things all wrapped up in this one person who also represented fear, shadows, and darkness. How do I begin to unwrap the complexities of this person who lived an entire life before I was even born? He is and has always been a puzzle but one where not all the pieces fit and some were missing entirely. I know a few intricate and sad details of his young life and those have, in moments, helped grow my understanding of the 'whys'. To help create a reason for the darkness he seemed to easily fall into. At times, he seemed to be a prisoner of it as much as we were.

He was thirty-seven when I was born and had married my mom just nine months before. I used to do the math over and over in my head. On the darkest of days in my room, when I was wishing for an escape from it all, I would wonder and hope that maybe I wasn't his. Maybe that would account for the shame I carried and the deeply rooted pain I felt just being near him. I would never have been surprised to have one day discovered that little seed of truth, but it never came. That math always added up to there being me even if I didn't want it to. I know I was wanted, I know there was love, but I didn't know it then. Those years in between the knowing and not knowing were where his darkness used up all the light.

He had just been a boy. He was a son and a brother, and later a man with ghosts, but he had only been a boy when his father left for war because he chose to. That terrible war made people walk away from family because it meant something more, his father chose to leave. He left a wife, that boy, and an even younger girl for many years. The wife also had to leave every day to go to work and that little boy and the girl were left with an aunt and uncle who had their own set of shadows kept hidden away in the dark. The girl was brought indoors and smothered with love, food, and warmth. The boy was left outside. He was left in the cold with his uncle who had been left out there too and he spent those days unsure and unsafe.

The uncle was an angry man, and a drunken one too. The boy was mistreated by both people whom the mother had trusted. Or perhaps she was never sure if she did but didn't allow herself to uncover the truth of it. The boy has always believed she had no choice and he loved her.

That little boy. He was never invited in. The detailed story of it all is not one I can share. In truth I don't even know the whole of it. I am not even certain he does either anymore. I have wondered what happened all those years ago out in the cold, alone and forgotten with the uncle who was alone and forgotten too. The perfect portrait of generational trauma played out during a dark time.

I believe that the boy's consciousness chose to live in a bubble outside the knowledge of what that time was like and that has led me here. Writing this memoir, journaling the darkness, and living through to today have been because of that boy. I write this today because of the darkness and the light and the shadows. They have been his story and that story has been slowly bleeding into my own, rippling out from the forgotten center and begging to escape. Growing further from it because he couldn't. He never learned how. I think I had to do it for both of us. Someone else had to see past it all. Someone had to see the puzzle from high above. To see the picture past the cracks and blurred edges, smudged colors and dark corners. To take note of the pieces that had yet to be put together. To see how they would align and create a whole person. A person healing and taking shape so all the pieces can finally fit.

Polliwogs

On those days, he was only my dad and I felt precious for a minute. The little boy and the ghosts didn't exist. When it was still and quiet, in those moments, I would hold my breath, that nothing would change the scene. If he laughed or smiled, the clouds lifted, the darkness had no space to be, and I could exhale. When the sun was bright and the day was new, he would suggest the adventure and on those days, nothing was better.

Those polliwogs. He loved looking for them, and with me. I was so happy when he wanted to take me. When the weather was warm enough on a Saturday and Spring was taking its turn to brighten up the days, we would gear up with our oldest sneakers, worn out jeans and journey to the pond. This was our own little project and I wasn't going to miss a moment of his wanting to be with me. There was no scorn or correction, only directions and giggles. It felt warm and safe there.

We discovered the polliwogs in the places he knew they would be. We collected them in a jar so I could take them home. We would borrow them for their journey from polliwog to tiny frogs. He would allow me to take care of them, talk to them, to simply just watch them grow. The day before our polliwog hunts, we would prepare the fish tank in the side yard where I could often be found making mud pies, or crafting perfume out of rose petals. Together we would design the temporary home for their beautiful evolution with carefully chosen rocks, decor to make it pretty, and we made sure they had plenty of food too.

I greeted them every morning running eagerly outside in my pajamas to see if they had changed from the day before. I told them stories from my days at school, sang to them, and loved watching them change from these heads with tails into tiny little frogs. Once they were big enough to be set free, Dad and I would once again, don our gear and take them back to the same spots we found them. We would say goodbye, leave them to continue to grow and evolve, and walk away hand in hand.

Later on, as I would begin to put together this intricate puzzle with its jagged edged pieces, I would cling to those polliwog hunting days. Once every early spring, my dad placed moments of good into his Darkness that was always lying in wait. In those early days, in the 'not knowing', I was never too confined or so terrified that I would forget those crisp spring mornings and warm days filled with the changing of those polliwogs. There was always just enough goodness and light. The heaviness of being weighed down with shame, beginning to question my role in his dark shadows, those darker days were yet to be. Polliwog's days were simple and surreal when looking back on the bigness of what was to come.

The years ahead would lead me to blame myself for the Dark that inevitably came. As a little girl who wanted to feel precious on more than polliwog days, to be held and given space, I would look up to my dad in those Spring days, hoping he was really seeing me, giving us both a little warmth and light. Those days, I believe, were a gift. Unknowingly, those Polliwog hunting days became what I would hold fast too when the days grew dark. It became a holding fast to something light and wonderful. Those days lived somewhere between the beginning and the middle of all that came to shape and create me. Just like those polliwogs I loved.

Part 1
Beginnings

Beginnings are all about the setup; the development. A timeline that makes the middle enticing and leads to the twists and turns that create a spectacular ending. The beginnings of our family were seemingly light, with only glimpses into times that were to come. The memories of good things in the beginning live with me still and I can recall many joy-filled days.

First Glimpses
Dott Court

Our first home lives only in a memory bank from old family movies. The kind of movie watching that was a complete sensory experience; the lights going dim, the sounds of the projector clicking on, the smells of the antique system awakening and making the screen jump while counting down to the beginning. I loved it all. They were my favorite nights at home, the good nights, move nights. Recollecting all the happiness that was kept like a treasure on that screen kept the light where I could see it. The buttery popcorn goodness greeted my taste buds while Dad captured each visual moment recalling it with a story. Whether it was toddling around the driveway pulling a favorite toy or seeing myself eating bologna and cheese in my highchair, the scenes were familiar, but not tangible. Some moments were of my brother, Jeff, who lived with us for a time and then didn't, ever again.

With his in-and-out existence living with his dad in another state, I was at first the youngest child when I was born as he was there. I claimed the oldest seat when my sister was born years later as he was away, and then there were the few visits from him that at times put me in the middle. That was before he never came back.

This home, I remember as a quieter version of the rest. It was smaller than those that would come later on, and a place where a little girl placed her first moments in a cloud of fuzzy warmth, or at least it seemed from that grand movie screen storytelling. I wish I could visualize more and sometimes ache to fill in the blank spaces. Those wonderful movie nights told joyful stories of that little house, but I was told much later that the Darkness took form there.

That dark chaos began shortly after my parents' wedding vows. They met through my great grandmother who was a woman ahead of her time. She was fierce and fiery and managed the apartment building my dad was living in. My mom came to visit one summer day after a divorce from a terrible man. Of course, my great-grandmother had plotted their meeting and after only a short period of time getting to know one another, they were married on Valentine's Day 1974. He was an ex-Navy pilot working for an airline. She was 11 years his junior, beautiful, willing, and with a little boy to care for. She needed the stability he offered. They had a small intimate ceremony and began a new life. They moved into the little rancher on Dott Ct. and nine months later, I was taking my first breath.

Soon after, on a morning when an infant would not stop crying, it came and never left. Dad became something that would be feared for my entire childhood. That crying baby brought a rage, a darkness, that lived most days in a quiet corner. The Darkness would hide and sneer and wait. On this first morning, in this little house, where so many other good things happened, he showed who he was in the shadows. In this little house where the movie camera caught all the memories that I would love watching on that screen on those perfect movie nights, it would seem the truth was silenced, not remembered. The truth was never on that screen or in those movies and that morning, there was a little one that could not be controlled.

That morning when he gave himself over to the Dark, when he shook and hit that baby and screamed for it to stop. When he slapped its mother for trying to intervene. When she was brave for the first and last time as she raised her voice and said, "NO." When he turned to her with that darkness in his eyes and said, "If you don't like the way I do things, you can leave."

When that moment happened, all the shadows grew in the hollows and were welcomed. She was silenced and scared and he became a powerful force and a controlling hand. Those shadows were granted light and the Dark was given permission to make a home and join the family.

Landerwood Lane

This was my favorite childhood home. Though this is where the darkness began to shape our family, I have so many fond memories that I am haunted by even more. This home placed me as oldest and middle child until oldest became my forever title.

Backyard Play

I recall the sunniest of days spent in our backyard as if it were a home all its own. It would keep us warm in the apple trees, protect us with its gated boundaries, fly us to the sky in its wonderful swings, and take us to other worlds as we would make-believe the days away. The outside was more of a home than the inside when the walls grew darker.

Those cheerful Easter egg hunts hiding the familiar and colorful plastic eggs filled with candy and goodness. I would hide the eggs, well more exactly, I would line them up in a row for my sister to easily find and place in her own basket. We were lucky enough to have a few apple, and cherry trees and one was the biggest and best umbrella tree of them all. We spent hours swinging and singing, picnicking, blowing bubbles, having tea parties with our stuffed animals and cabbage patch dolls.

That yard gleamed hours of rolling out the slip and slide on those hot, lazy summer days, creating perfumes from the soft petals we would collect, making too many mud pies to count, and catching butterflies to see them up close and then let them fly away again. I loved that yard and I loved those moments. The Light was playful there. The Dark couldn't find us if we were laughing and being little girls on those outdoor imagination-filled days in the sun.

Bubbles and Bikes

The front yard was a magic all its own, always covered with messy olive tree remnants and somehow that was perfect. The inside was not covered with remnants as easy to clean up as what the pesky olive tree left behind. Outside was safer, cleaner in its messiness, a sweet and good place to be. The front porch was covered and shielded with tall bushes. It ran the length of the front of the house and became an extension of my room for playing school or reading on rainy fall mornings.

I learned how to ride a bike in the front yard with my dad's help and when we would share the space on other days it was usually about car washing. I would chase the bubbles from our driveway all the way along the sidewalk and down to the drain. Talking to those bubbles while they made their escape became my routine while Dad would wash and shine the cars. I learned to be careful and fearful of things here too. I was afraid of stepping on the cracks in the sidewalk. I would hop over each one until one bubble chasing day, I just forgot to care. I learned to be afraid of bike riding once I graduated to my brother's bike that had been left behind and was now mine to use. I was afraid because stopping the bike was a part of riding it and I couldn't seem to grasp that as well. I remember the day I allowed the prickly bush at the end of my street to stop my momentum. I remember that learning to ride that blue bike seemed awkward and out of place as it had been meant for him. He had left long before, but this piece of him was leftover and I was supposed to feel safe riding it. I would ride it and be hopeful that I wouldn't be sent away too. Family bike riding was a slow passage of time for us back then, when things felt lighter and simpler, when Saturday's meant sunshine and adventure on bikes. We would leave in the morning and I would ride that blue bike as best as I could with Dad leading the way. I wish I had known then to grasp hold of and keep close these simple moments in those sacred spaces. I wish I had known to store them all up in a treasure box to be visited again and again when the days of Darkness would take all the light away for a while.

Sundays

Sundays were Grandma days. I felt treasured, safe, and loved when we were with her. We would take her to church and then join her at her home for pastry treats and our Sunday family meal. Many afternoons were spent at the pool with us all enjoying time in the sun and in the water. I stayed very close to the edge in the water, but it was still so calming and cool nevertheless. She made Sundays so lively and lovely. Maybe because she was joy; grounded and tolerant. I remember playing with her pop bead jewelry in the backseat of the car. I remember the smell of her condo and the way I was wrapped up in its safety every Sunday when the Darkness was beginning to keep watch within our own walls. I remember sitting on her back patio on summer days watching for hummingbirds and butterflies to dance around us. I remember her gentle words of warning if my dad mis-spoke or became angry at some child-like behavior.

I remember when a lamp was broken one evening out of carelessness and the Darkness entered her house too. Her light always warded off the Dark. She was magic. I remember when she was sick and cared for and after many years of painful suffering, passed away. She was our guardian angel on Sundays and carried with her all the light possible. She may have just carried all of the light there ever was inside of her.

A New Name

Dad was a pilot and had been since his early 20's. Beginning in the Navy, he flew because he lived for it. He told me once that he had such lifelike dreams of flying through the sky, soaring like a bird, he had just known he was meant to be in flight. I have always wondered if flying kept the Darkness at bay more often than we knew or whether the perfection of being a pilot prompted its coming. When he arrived back home after a week away, we faced the weekends with hope for more than what they were becoming if not with Grandma, but with trepidation of what they often became if the Darkness decided to visit.

Dad usually made all the weekend plans and if we did anything outside the walls of home, they were of his design. We frequented a restaurant almost weekly that had been our place for years and for many more to come. The Darkness was something I was becoming more aware of now. I knew where it lived and would anxiously anticipate its arrival. But I knew that coming here was a place only the light would show and we could just be the family we wanted to be. My dad was accustomed to eating out regularly being away from home so often. Service was important to him out of necessity and he got the best here. He was royalty. Everyone knew him, loved him, and cheered when we would walk through the door. High praise, I realize now, was what kept him functioning without having to dive deep into those dark corners. My parents had spent many meals here even before I was born. If it was a place my dad liked, then that's where we would be. The story told to me was that when my parents would come to dine when I was an infant, I was carried around by the staff so they could enjoy a quiet meal. As we grew, this place became an extended version of our own dining room. We would learn the stories of anyone who served us our meal and the meal was always the same; steak, potatoes and salad drenched in blue cheese. There was one part of this weekly journey that began to bring darkness here too. The Lodge had a statue upon entrance, a dark brown wooden statue that looked angry. Its expression began to match my own feelings arriving here as I grew older and more aware of the Darkness. My dad chose this statue to be my look alike… He would liken me to his sour expression, moody attitude, and enjoyed reminding of it every time we pulled in the parking lot. The statue in fact was given a name that had unfortunately also been my nickname for years. As a little girl, my dad decided he would call me his 'little wort'. He delighted in the fact that I was unable to pronounce that and named myself 'Little bort' instead. It doesn't really mean anything, it never did. It could have been a good name, but the meaning behind it was not. Darkness had decided long ago that it would be a daily reminder that I was not sunshine, or a bright light, never just enough, and on that day, when the Darkness designated this statue and me to be one and the same, he decided that everything wrapped up in that silly name would exist visually too. Our visits to the Lodge, this place that had once felt safe and warm because it wasn't home, became another reminder that I wasn't enough. I was reminded with each visit. Every entry into the parking lot became the beginning of the dark in a place that used to be light. Dad would make sure to let me know when we passed the statue that it looked like me. I don't remember feeling hungry enough to eat that steak and potato and salad drenched in blue cheese anymore, but we continued to visit weekly, and that statue was always there reminding me that the Darkness was everywhere.

The Dining Room

I remember the thrill of childhood birthdays. The hours my mom spent on those special days designing a glorious birthday table in the dining room and it always seemed to take a lifetime. The magic doors that separated the living room from the dining room would remain closed all day long. The sounds of shuffling feet preparing the room for its festivities kept me anticipatory. Mom would work tirelessly on those meals, the decor, the cake, and I am quite certain the presents too. I always requested spaghetti or lasagna and the cake was a fun surprise for everyone and intricately woven together with her skilled hands. Of course the dining room was not always for birthday dinners, we came together many evenings for Mom's amazing food and the view out the slider to my sanctuary of a backyard. Grandma would be there for many meals and sometimes my other grandparents too. In my memories it seemed as though any wonderfully light filled place would always leave just enough space for the darkness to create a pathway inside of it. The space that my sister and I occupied at the table always had to be prepared and so did we. A towel was laid down for the eminent messes, bibs were worn to protect our clothes, and a ponytail had to be worn at every meal so food was not left as a remnant to be washed out later. Perfection at the table seemed to be how every family meal began. Birthdays included.

I recall one evening that my dad came to the carefully prepared table wearing bright red lipstick, dangly earrings, and some of my clips in his hair. It could have been a birthday dinner or an everyday dinner, I can't recall. He thought it was hilarious, did it for attention, and who knows what else. He laughed for so long and I was completely terrified, confused, concerned, and ran away from the table. There were rules for us at the table, we waited for everyone to sit down before we started eating, we asked nicely for things to be passed or to have seconds, and we always had to ask to be excused. This particular night of his showcase was so uncharacteristic of my dad's need for keeping tidy, it was so beyond anything we had ever seen him do. He never did it again but recalls the story with laughter that I never could understand. Though we have brought up the story many times as a family, he still thinks it was one of his better showings and retells the story as though he may have done it just to get the reaction out of me that he did. I still don't know what actually prompted it or why he chose to do it, but I do know that after that I was even more unsure of the trust I could place in my dad to ever hold me close enough in his heart for me to trust him with mine. The Darkness rolled in slowly, but with fierceness nonetheless. Those polliwog hunting days were fading to a sunrise past, one that I would remember fondly and cry out for long after it was gone. The dining room became a circus of confusion;

rules, and sometimes the Darkness sat with us at the table. Those stories at the table came later, the shadows were just beginning to taunt and play back then. I think my dad has lived his life confused, wounded, and terrified of the dark corners within. The dining room was a place where we often saw those emotions played out like it was a stage for our family only. The rest of the world wasn't invited in, they were often kept out. It was just easier that way. Someone else may have been able to see behind the shadows to the Darkness that only we knew existed there.

Just Words

Greeting cards. The idea of them is lovely and my parents, and perhaps mostly my dad, loved them. He still does. To this day he spends hours searching for the perfectly written greeting card and I have a terrible time rummaging through the selection anywhere I am looking for one to give. We all knew that the day before any holiday, birthday or Mother's Day, Dad would leave the house for most of the afternoon to search for and collect his versions of truth in a greeting card. With the knowledge of what they represented to me and how the words inside would often mask what I believed the truth really was in our home, they were and still can be triggering. In this home and the others yet to come, I recall that every holiday there were envelopes with my mother's name on them waiting to be opened and tearfully read. He would leave them, she would read them, and when she left a card for him, he would read it aloud in front of us all and she would then recite hers as well. Maybe she thought it was expected by him, another way to appease the

Darkness. Perhaps she did it for herself, but regardless, it was an event that we all had to take notice of. He was so proud of what he had gone and out and collected, like they were a shiny prize that he was to be acknowledged for discovering on his own. It never mattered what words had been said the day before or what actions had followed, they would read the heartfelt words and tearfully thank one another and reach for each other's embrace. I would sit, and watch, and wonder; how was this Darkness, this thing that I was now old enough to be aware of, able to tearfully give of himself so lovingly in a singular moment, and also live the rest of them; demanding, intolerant, incapable of relationship without strings, angry at tears or frustration, and watching our every movement for stumbling and mistakes when he was home. I could not make sense of their tears in these moments, not when I could sense everything else. The words they spoke out loud every day were not the words that they searched for in those greeting cards. At one point, we were all expected to read our cards aloud, especially during holiday gift giving, and the words in those cards, written by someone else, always held more weight than the gift being given. If only the actions from my dad spoke more loudly than the words that he prided himself on searching so endlessly to find inside those overpriced and poetically phrased words that were nothing like our real life.

The Hallway

What I really remember in my darkest of days was the hallway. The long, green floral, 70s wallpapered hallway that spanned from the garage entrance to the small bathroom off the kitchen. That hallway felt cold, dark and terrifying one particular summer of my childhood. I was 5 and my sister and I were taking our first swim lessons. She was a fish out of water at 2 years old in her bright pink swimsuit and ready for anything. I was not. Scared beyond belief, I went to the lessons every day, each one as horrible or worse than the day before. My dad had threatened spankings when I got home if I didn't get in the water and do what they asked me too. I tried not to be afraid. I was desperate for that feeling of freedom my little sister possessed.

Each day, after the lessons ended, I knew what I had tempted out of the shadows. The dread and anticipation began the moment I made my way to the car and the ride home was agonizing. I walked the long walk down that hallway and waited. My mom would tell me to go and I would. My mom was okay with this story and okay with the aftermath. Maybe she was afraid too. Maybe the lesson, the car ride and telling me to walk down the hallway was agonizing for her too. I wanted so badly to be adored by him, but it just never seemed possible.

The Darkness became real that summer. I knew it was my dad, but he felt like a different person. He was angry at me, as though my fear was a punishment to him, that I was afraid on purpose. As though I wanted to cry at the pool every day and feel the shame in my fear of what I had to do. There was nothing I could do to get away, or explain how I felt, to even have a voice for my fear. How does a little girl explain all of that? I knew that he blamed me, for all of it; his threats, his anger, and my punishment were all my fault. Everything that was wrong with me and everything about me he couldn't tolerate brought the shadows out to play.

I was a naughty little girl and there just wasn't enough goodness no matter how good I believed I was. I was there, with him, bent over the toilet, cold from the wet of the pool drying on my skin, underwear down, and a ruler in my side view. Every day of those summer swim lessons was the same, weeks with shame and darkness. After the spankings, he would leave in a fit of anger and I was left in that little bathroom down that ugly green hallway, confused, misunderstood, and helpless for a voice to cry out with.

Everything changed for me that summer. The Darkness had unfurled, slithered out from the shadows and never left. It would hide away for bits of time and safety felt tangible, and then it was dark again.

Cindy Doll

Christmas was joy, in this home anyway. I can still picture myself coming into the living room when my parents called my sister and I from our rooms. Dressed in Christmas jammies and two swinging ponytails, I would float down the hallway knowing that the moments were few now before I would see what had been left out by Santa and then, there she was, dressed in a white top, blue pants, donning the cutest blond ponytails, and she was mine. I adored her from day one. She was a life-size version of friendship with the very best of names.

I knew she wasn't real, of course, but she was always smiling. I was rather fascinated by that. One day after arriving home from school, I went to tell her all the things that had happened that day. I opened my closet door where she was kept so as not to make the room untidy, but she was gone. Frantically, I asked my mom where she was. I just knew I had left her where she would be safe while I was away. She wasn't coming back. Mom had decided it was time to give her away to someone else, but I knew the real reason she was gone.

The Darkness had visited that day. I must have left her out when I thought I had put her away. Dad had become frustrated and angry that I would leave her out sometimes and my room couldn't be as clean as we were told to keep it. Mom had relented to his unhappiness and had decided to give her away just like that. I was devastated and I wanted to grieve the loss of my friend, but I knew the more sad I appeared, the worse the Darkness would become and the more like that ugly brown statue I would be.

Sunday Tights

Sunday church mornings and tights went hand and hand. Dressing in our best meant pulling those things up and up and up some more. They never seemed to want to stay where they were supposed to, no matter how much I was after them to do so. I despised Sunday morning tights and the test of endurance it was to wear them. Tights also meant the worry over tearing them, getting a hole in them, snagging them, and getting them dirty, especially if it was a white tights Sunday. All of that was simply too easy to do.

Tights are designed to make little girls fail miserably, little girls and tights don't mix and when the Darkness came to visit this particular morning, everything about tight Sunday was just a whole lot worse. They were red, too old, too itchy, too small, and I had stayed in them a little too long. Playing after church in my room and on my knees, they grew weak in one spot and one tiny hole grew much bigger and that led to an afternoon alone in my room. Perhaps they had told me to take them off when we got home and I didn't so it was my fault. Perhaps, that is why the Darkness was so angry about tights and so angry about me too.

Stars

Before Sister was born, and maybe before my brother left too, Dad would take me outside when the sky was glowing with its nighttime artistry. He would pick me up, point to the sky, and tell me stories of all that we could see. I was too young to understand it all, but I knew that being there with him felt safe and warm. I didn't question the moments when he saw me as precious, I ached for them. He would explain the names of things he knew up in the sky. I would call them 'tars' and he would laugh, bold and big as I would come to know his laugh to be on light-filled days, and he would call them 'tars' too.

When he took me out at night to talk about the stories in the sky, I never minded the darkness above, never felt alone or afraid. When his Darkness was away, it was always good, and right, and enough. I came to learn that the beauty of a still moment was to be acknowledged because the next might become chaos. It's been decades now, and time is a funny thing; a great commodity and a tease. The reaching for and wanting more, hoping for different, have eased. The roles we play in our families, our marriages, and our circles all stem from reaching towards both. Darkness did not strive for those things in a way that would better itself. Dad simply didn't know how to acknowledge that he needed too. He did, of course, hope that I would.

In his eyes, I wasn't born good enough, you have to work for that. Wanting more and expecting different didn't lend itself to being good enough. It was later that I would learn, moments with him were not a safe guard or a promise of love without strings. The stars were looking down on me that night and sighing with defeat as they appeared to twinkle while I leaned into the quiet. They knew that the future would mean years of his lasting Darkness inside and how he would affect everyone in the family because of it.

Two-Headed Worms

The uniforms weren't terrible. I rather liked them. I never felt concerned over having to wear them or be seen in them and everyone looked the same in their skirts and knee highs and living in that uniform everyday was a safe space to be in. A controlled environment in clothing was my elementary school experience until about the middle of 5th grade. During that time, I remember spending every minute I could with my best friend. He was the greatest thing beyond bologna and cheese.

Chad—I just adored his blond hair and blue-eyed face. We spent all of our early elementary school days chasing recess as if we could catch it and exist within it. We searched high and low every day of second grade looking for special worms on the bushes that I could have sworn to anyone (and did) that those ugly things had two heads. Each side of its body moved as though it couldn't make up its mind where it began and ended. They were magic.

No matter what Chad and I ended up doing at recess, I would always check in on those worms and in my head I could never quite figure them out. I told my dad about them one day and of course, there was no end to the mockery. It was all in good fun I told myself, but I sure didn't believe it when he insisted they didn't actually own two heads. From one end to the other, they had no face, no eyes to see, no end to their beginning. I pondered at how much they must have to miss out on and how in fact, did they get to where they were hoping to go?

When the Darkness would arrive and settle in for a stay, I would find solace in the routine of donning that uniform, finding Chad, catching recess, and looking for those worms every day. I decided that it was okay that I couldn't figure them out and it was certainly okay if they did in fact have two heads. Kind of like my dad, he felt like the two-headed worm sometimes. Confused about his darkness and in conflict over who he was, I knew he was mine to love regardless, just like those worms, and Chad, and recess, and the safety of that uniform. I decided I would love him as hard as I could. I decided I could learn to love in the darkness. Thank goodness for my first friend Chad, recess, knee-high socks and those silly two-headed worms. Loving was so much easier when I could leave the Darkness at home and soak in the magic of school days.

The Red Swings

I just could never be high enough. It was like flying in those beautiful red swings. A gift from my dad, on a day he was light and free. I wonder if he knew that he was giving me those same things whenever I ran to them, sat in them, and pushed and pulled to find the sky. They supported me, grounded me and let the sunshine pour over me. Sister and I couldn't find enough hours in the day to soak in them. My backyard haven had become a literal sanctuary. In the spring, those red swings would tempt us when the dew was still on the grass and the temperature was too chilly to play, but we didn't care.

Out we would go with towels to wipe off the morning mist and jackets to keep us warm. Sister would start on her belly and I would get my legs moving as hard and as fast as they could. I wanted the height of those stars at night and the weightless drop on the other side. That one moment when you're as high as you can possibly go and you are about to begin the drop back down again. It was light and it was freedom. No Darkness could find me on those swings; in those skyward moments where the sun's warmth and the breeze, together would carry away all that wasn't light. Freedom was a delicious feeling.

In the summer, we would race to see who could get to them first. I suppose we had our favorite even though there were only two. One for my sister and one for me. It felt as though once our bodies had positioned and designed one seat to be just right, we didn't want the other. We ran anyway, to get there faster, to find that freedom sooner, to be carefree and warm and light up in the sky. Once we discovered how much fun it was to swing while singing, my time on those red swings was never-ending. From Madonna to Disney, we would give free and unwanted concerts to the whole neighborhood. During those warmer months, we would often forget that though beautifully red, they were also rubber seats and would leave behind their remnants representing the time spent on them. Sister and I would then endure the torture of having to have tiny red shavings taken out of the backs of tanned summer legs. We quickly learned that placing a towel over their beautiful seats was an absolute must.

Later when we left that home for the next, leaving those swings was so terribly hard. If I had understood their importance back then, it would have been devastating. I suppose everyone leaves behind tidbits of childhood in moments when they don't even realize it. The simple gift of them that my dad gave was treasured and used. A gift that he never knew the importance of or how much I needed it and neither did I back then. When the sun warmed me and the breeze carried me, it was Light, and it was good. Darkness was never on the swings or in the songs, or out with the birds or in the early morning summer dew. I learned early on to hold close the importance of small moments and little things.

The Magic of Rainy Days

The late months of winter into spring were dreary when I was young. I missed the comforts of outside and encouragement it would give. Instead of the solace of the sun, Sister and I spent hours inside crafting forts that Mom would help us design. Cozy and secure we would gather our games, stuffed animals, books, and whatever else we could find to create magic with and just be. Some nights we even rolled out the sleeping bags, pillows, and popcorn, and slept there too. At least until we were too afraid to last in the dark.

Fort days were full of play and the lazy keeping of time. Light was with us too, the military-esque rules were bent a little and the mess was okay within those blanketed walls as long as Dad was away. Sister and I had two favorite games with us on days of warmth in the rain and we played them so many times, unencumbered by the monotony that came with it. We would giggle when Sister would leave her obvious Old Maid card higher than all the rest hoping that I would choose it. Once I caught on to her plan, I would trick her by leaving the card next to the Old Maid higher. She would be so irritated when she would end up with the unwanted card over and over again. What began as a civil and childish game of cards, quickly led to many arguments over fairness.

Inevitably, we would give up on that game and switch to the other. The number of times she would turn the game board on its head over being returned home, were many. She was joy-filled and vibrant. A wonderful little being, and I adored her. So did Dad. He loved her with this beautifully gracious 'enough-ness' and I was enthralled by it. I ached for it. All his praise, joy, and soft expressions seemed to be all used up. I was not angry or jealous of his attention and praise given her way, I just wanted to be able to feel that enough-ness. I wanted to be different than I was to earn it all too. Maybe then the Darkness would fade into Light. Maybe then all the forts, and backyard play, swings and

Grandma Sundays, could just be those simple things. Or maybe all those things were meant to be there to show me peace and comfort because this was always the plan.

Maybe the plan had always included the puzzle pieces of the Darkness and the Light. I learned to soak in the benefit of knowing how to create places that I could find and escape too. I knew to keep the rainy days as a blanket to wrap myself in to make sure I remembered that the inside was okay. To remember that all the insides of ME were okay too. Darkness stayed with us too long and became too unpredictable to keep my insides that safe in the years to come.

Losing Grandma

Then one ordinary day, she just wasn't okay. She was life in all its miraculous forms and she was losing hers, one little moment at a time. We watched as she withered away and listened as she cried out. She was an angel losing her earthly wings and we were helpless to do anything but graciously say goodbye. Visiting her was a weekly ritual and a difficult one too. Sister and I made the best of our many hours in her nursing home. We sang and danced when we thought no one was watching to pretend to be anywhere else. We did our best to not to be afraid when we walked past others who were lost within themselves.

We tried our best to interact with Grandma and hoped she would continue to remember who we were. We held her hand and talked softly to her until she would cry out again and we would have to leave. We would try to help her eat, but then she started to refuse it. The night she left us for heaven's embrace, I was lying awake in my room knowing that my dad had left hours earlier to see her. He hadn't taken us with him. I couldn't sleep, I felt her with me, but I couldn't find peace with that. He came home and to my bedside to tell me himself that she was gone. He had stayed with her and held her and loved her until she had lived her very last moment. He left my room and went to his own, where my mom waited for him. The tears shed from my dad were frightening and loud, hopeless and mournful. I had never seen him vulnerable and transparent before. He was without both parents then and I remember wondering if I would cry like that for him someday.

It took me hours to fall asleep that night listening to his weeping as she consoled and soothed him. My safe place was gone, taken, and I longed for her. I still long for her. With her, the Darkness was kept at bay, quieted and challenged. I was afraid of what her passing would do to the Light that was left. A change was coming, a shifting of shadows, and a more frequent invitation for the Darkness to reside.

Part 2
In the Middle

"There will be a boy around every corner!" For some reason, Dad assumed this would make the transition to a new city, new schools, and a new home an hour away from the old one, seemingly easier to bear. I do recall that this move didn't seem to scare me as much as it thrilled me. Our new home was a two-story house. I was completely unfamiliar with the concept of having a staircase in a home that I had lived in and that seemed to make everything okay for a moment.

The boy thing, on the other hand, I was unsure of why I needed to be ready for that. Up until this moment, I had only ever known a boy named Chad. My friend who created a safe haven while looking for two-headed worms and swimming in Grandma's pool. I missed him and knew that I always would. I never did see him again after the move and I don't remember our last day together. Did we say goodbye? Did I tell him thank you for believing that those worms had two heads? How could I understand then that leaving people often meant that their role in your existence would never be the same? They simply were not a part of you anymore.

Our time in each other's lives was simply over. There was a lot of 'missing' in the car that day; missing Chad, missing the swings and the tadpoles, missing Grandma, and missing what I knew of life with the Darkness when she was guarding us from it. I didn't know if the Darkness was still with us. I knew I was hopeful that it had been left behind with old memories. I wish I could have prepared the younger me for the coming of darker shadows in the days ahead.

The Brown House

It seemed ironic that we pulled up to a house that looked like this one. Its two eye-like windows above the garage made it seem as though the house was always watching. We were used to eyes on us and being watched. Its color was also a daily reminder of a familiar statue and a reminder to me every day of how I was seen when I was watched. Aside from the irony of it all, Sister and I had our own space in the house, and for the first time, the idea of a hallway was a wonderful thing. We walked up the stairs, passed my parents' room and down a long hallway. A hallway with a left turn at the end of it that housed both of our rooms, and our own bathroom too.

We lived above the watchful eyes of the house, but it felt separated, safe and away from the Dark. The living room was large with plenty of room for the piano my dad would purchase in the future and the gold couch too. There were beautiful big windows that looked out on the front yard that I would quickly learn would bring its own love/hate relationship for me. The kitchen was a room of its own and had a pass-through window to the back patio where we would spend many evenings dining al fresco and enjoying the view of the golf course and the pond where two mated swans would draw us into their world every spring and summer. A few steps below the kitchen eating area was our family room where TV-watching and awkward family evenings at home would take place.

The slider to the backyard would lead to many summer nights in the hot tub and keeping warm from the chilly Northern California morning fog by the fire. This is where I grew up over the next 6 years. A strength was unlocked, wishes and dreams were given life, and pivotal experiences would lead to growth. The quilt of my life was being pieced together one small patch at a time. and the Darkness would continue to weave its way through it all.

Heartfelt Pants

I wish I could go back in time and make them some semblance of a great thing, like those pants that traveled from friend to friend and around the world to create magic in the lives of those who wore them. I wanted so badly for those pants to make me feel light and wonderful every time I wore them and they did until they didn't. All the feelings came with those pants with small hearts of color all over them. In them, I felt wanted, warm, tender, and seen a little too. They were certainly magic to me.

My school year in our new home began halfway through 5th grade within new and unfamiliar walls. A public school where the kids were louder, there were no uniforms, and no two headed worms. New faces were abundant and the attitudes about the new girl were less than welcoming. This was hard. Two girls in particular did not make things anywhere near enjoyable. Creating drama around everything and anything, including me, was their daily practice. Mocking my style, my friends, my unfortunate permed hair, and the fact that I was in choir that year were just a few of the things they loved to remind me of. I appreciated the outcasts; the ones who didn't have a home base. I was okay with being in the shadowy corners and surviving the rest of the year, except for one thing.

My new teacher, Mr. T, was the best and the first male teacher I had ever had. He created a classroom of unconditional acceptance and wasn't afraid to override the ideals hiding in the shadowy corners that seem to come with being new and disregarded. The day came, when 'the pants' made their appearance in my world and my 5th grade life changed the moment they did. For better and for worse, they were the best thing ever and instantly created joy back in my new world. Those pants invited me into their safekeeping and I lived in them for that, almost every day. Until, that is, the day those two girls decided that I must never wash my clothes, and to relay that rumor back to everyone.

Embarrassing doesn't begin to describe how I perceived their rantings and cruel mockery. They were destroying that safety net, that happiness, that every day comfort. For a while, they did, until they didn't. Until I decided I just loved those pants too much to keep them at home forever just for the sake of avoiding humiliation. Granted, I did decide to rotate them on a once a week time frame and share the love with some others clothes too. Eventually, the embarrassment over clothing choices refrained from rearing its ugly head for the remainder of the school year. I seemed to settle in to the new and the messages from Mr. T became stronger towards those bullies. The safety and warmth I felt when I wore those pants was a gift for the time I needed it.

The new school, the new classroom, the new house with the two watching eyes. The newness of being known again was terrifying and I just longed for a safe space away wearing the most wonderful pants in the world that was light filled without any room for the Dark. I knew it was only a matter of timing and circumstance until the Darkness would show itself in this new place. I was just glad those heartfelt pants, my sadness, and confusion from those two bullying girls had not brought it out of the shadows.

His Name Was Brett

He was a 6th-grader and I thought he was just the best thing in my world after I had worn out my magic pants. My dad may have been kidding about boys around every corner, but my heart was feeling the first twinges of a first crush. Brett was tall, a 6th grader, and didn't know I existed. What with my braces, ponytails, and those pants, I'm sure I had really stood out. Maybe he had heard the rumors about me and the pants, or maybe the ponytail that was worn almost daily was to blame. Whatever it was left it much easier for me to ache over his presence while mine was shadowed within his comings and goings. The icing on the cake was the fact that he lived down the street in a cute little house that I had to pass almost daily on my walk home from school.

On one occasion, which is also now known as the day of my first heartbreak, I was walking by his house on my way home from school only to realize he was outside mowing the lawn. I decided to be so brave and stop my route home to talk with him since it would seem even more awkward to simply walk by and ignore him completely. He stopped the lawnmower and asked if I wouldn't mind picking up something that was on the grass in front of him and was decidedly in the way of his mowing. So, of course, because of the crush and because he was speaking to me, I stopped to pick it up and immediately realized I had been tricked. He was doubled over with laughter and shouting that I had almost picked up his dog's dried up old number two. I was embarrassed, humiliated and it didn't even matter that I had put those silly pants in my closet that day. I was so ashamed that I had been so ready to do anything for him that I didn't take notice of what I had in fact been ready to do. I was heartbroken.

I ran home in tears to discover that Dad was outside washing the car. He stopped me when I tried to run past him, and asked what had happened. I tearfully told my story, trying not to be too emotional as I did. I was desperate for him to tell me it was okay, to wrap me up in a warm blanket of empathy and understanding for a broken spirit. But he couldn't, or wouldn't, and I triggered the dark right out of the shadows. With the house watching it all, the Darkness came over him without warning. I could see it in his eyes as his face turned cold and terrifying as my story came to an end. I was painfully aware that I should have hidden my tears before arriving home and held my sorrow until I had found the safety of my own room all the way down that long hallway.

With his soapy sponge dripping cold, dirty water onto the pavement, he scolded me for making a scene and for allowing myself to be so 'boy-crazy' that I could have let it happen in the first place. The Darkness seemed to bounce in his angry veins as he watched my tears continue to fall now more so because the Darkness had returned. It was as though the sunny spring day had turned into a winter storm just over this brown house with its two window-like eyes watching it all.

Standing in shame, in tears in front of Dad and this dark brown house just reminded me what a moody girl I was and this was another example of how shameful those emotions were. I tried so hard to be strong, to make the tears stop, and to endure his tirade without allowing the messages to sink in. I felt so ashamed and immediately blamed myself for what had happened on such a routine, simple walk home.

As the Darkness became enraged by its own craze he stared at me with that look that was meant to frighten, to take emotional hostages, and to threaten. The threat was spoken low, under this breath. If I mentioned to Mom what he had said to me, He would leave the house, not be home for Easter that weekend, and I would be responsible for explaining why he wasn't there. I was the one to blame in his eyes, maybe for things I couldn't understand, maybe for reasons that he didn't either. I ran into the house, ran for air to breath that wasn't heavy from the toxic walk home. I wanted to run down that hallway for the walls of my room, my sanctuary.

The room that lived above those two watchful window eyes who had just seen it all. I tried to make it to my room without being seen, but my mom had heard the shouting and was already nearing the door. She knew the Darkness had come. Maybe she called it that too, I never knew. She was angry, not at me, but at her awareness of how the Darkness would visit us all and leave us victims of its rages. What had happened was beyond my secret keeping abilities and I was so wounded by it, that she could read me before I had a chance to get to my room. She could always do that back then.

They argued, because they did that now. Mom was stronger than she used to be, but the Darkness still won that day. I remember thinking that he should have left and been gone for Easter anyway, then the Darkness wouldn't have covered the light. I remembered thinking that the day could have played out so differently. I could have made a different choice when I passed by Brett's house. I could have walked home triumphantly and told a different version of the story.

But really, Dad could have chosen a different path too and ultimately he was the only reason the Darkness showed up that day. I know that now, I wasn't strong enough to know it then. I read in my room for hours after that. I read those books where you could choose your own ending. They were fascinating and my favorites. Why couldn't I have just flipped to a different page and chosen a different ending? I replayed the day's end so many times in my head as I tried to overcome the shame and guilt I was left with. I knew in my heart, the ending should have been so very different. I was stuck in an ending I didn't choose. The Darkness had returned, won, and it had been because of an

11year old girl's first broken heart. This was the first day in our new home that I had seen its return. That was a more heartbreaking reality than my own childish shame from that walk home and stopping to talk to that boy named Brett.

Evolution of Sundays

After the deep loss of Grandma and a transition to a new home and new city, Sundays had not been what they used to be. We slowly began to crawl towards a new version of the day than we had lived in a while. This day still began with time spent within a church that I was confused by, but a religion had Dad grown up in so we did too. A zippy trip down the highway in my dad's 1984 Camaro was the gesture of fun he would take us there in. There were gentlemanly manners that I would notice from him typically present on church morning. He would always open our doors for us and close them too and as much as he wanted to drive to and from with the top down in that car, he would always wait until after the service was over before doing so for the drive back home.

With wind-tossed hair, we would return and promptly pick up Mom for an afternoon out. Typically, we might drive as far as the Lodge for Sunday brunch for it was my dad who chose the destination, at every turn and of course the brown statue would greet us after we had left our brown house. Sometimes after dining, we would venture out in search of Open Houses. For whatever reason it seemed to be an activity we all enjoyed. Perhaps it allowed us a breath of light, fresh air. Maybe it was an opportunity to see without the clouds in the way.

The Darkness never left the house, you see. He was dormant in front of others and in the car. We could step into someone else's walls and moments were safe, normal, and seemingly full of Light. We would search and usually find several homes to step into, walk through, and see beautiful things in. I would find myself wishing for the unattainable feelings of More and Different as I carefully walked through each room. I went through each one until finding the room that would be my safe place if we lived there.

Of course, none of those rooms ever belonged to me, the temporary feeling of safety would dissolve the closer we came to returning to the brown house with the window eyes that watched. We would return, after a day away from the Darkness, and I would wonder how long it would be before it found us again.

Cave of Color

As time went on in the brown house, we delved into change; for me that meant middle school, and high school and still I continued to cling to the hope that my dad would magically become who I hoped he could be. His travel as a Pilot took him away several days of the week and then home again for the weekends. As I became older, the realization set in, that the weekdays were my favorite and my enemy all at the same time. The three of us left at home would grow into a new routine of school, work, and play and it was where all the Light was found. But as the days would pass much quicker than I would have liked, the lingering feelings of anxiousness lived within our walls. The knowledge that he was coming home and re-entering the family was always alarming. This family that had been joyful, carefree, and laughing were now struggling to live within the shadows we knew were always with us.

He would initially bring with him some hope that it could be a quiet weekend and I knew that if I could simply be compliant, agreeable, always grateful and non-emotional, all would be well and the Darkness would stay at bay. Soon he would learn of mistakes made while he was away, or child-like behavior that threatened his position of control and his overbearing voice as a Father who had not been home to 'lead'. He would be disappointed in a wife that did not take care of things the way they should have been. I remember Mom telling him many times that there were so many rules nobody could possibly keep them all straight. It was too much for us, too much for her, too much expectation for anyone.

Depending on what he felt needed to be 'fixed', the Darkness had the capacity to range from outlandish disciplining to a dramatic session of name calling, profanities and rage that would leave open wounds on every emotional surface. It often seemed that the walls themselves were soaking up all the despair as if to try and save us from bearing the weight of the intensity and the aftermath.

The repercussions of feelings that are not well described with words like fear, resentment, chaos, and confusion. Feelings that left me standing paralyzed in a puddle of muck not knowing what to do or where to escape and until much later would not know I needed to heal from. I did not really understand what I had lived in or that it was a Darkness he didn't even see within himself.

Once the Darkness came, it lived as if it were a whole other existence within our family, an extension of my dad that he wasn't even aware of. Like an extra person who was living and breathing among us. Trauma was the cave of color we lived in; all of us together. We didn't know that was what it was. We didn't know that was its name. I didn't know it could have been different. I don't know if any of us did. I just knew I desperately wanted it to be without being ungrateful for what was being provided.

It was the constant circus of knowing things were dark and light at the same time but knowing that our Darkness was a living being who was unaware of it. Unaware of the shadows that lurked in every home we were in as if they just waited for us to arrive. It was simply our 'normal'. While Sundays could be freeing, and Mondays meant we would have room to breathe, it was those in between days that caught me in a tumbling and rolling of anticipation and anxiousness. Our days of colorful cave living and hiding with a strained kind of hope, were where we existed on those days.

"Who lives here?" Is what Dad would say as we entered the garage after Open House viewings. Back to the brown house with the two window eyes that watched us. After our escape to other homes that he had determined were never greater than our own, we were all to agree that it just didn't look better than this anywhere else we had been. We would take his question and sort it through our own filters. My thoughts were lonely, fearful and always the same. I wondered if those homes were actually colorful caves on certain days too, and those families who lived there were learning to live in chaos when their own Darkness would visit. I hoped that wasn't true.

Bathroom Lunches

So the lovingly worn heart pants hadn't been a hit to anyone but me. I don't really even remember what happened to them, but I am, without a doubt, positive that they did not make it into my middle school fashion closet. 7th and 8th grade were heavy days. At this point, the Darkness at home was dreaded in every sense and now I faced a devastating reality during the school days as well. Bully's and cliques have historically been a disastrous pairing with middle school life and they certainly proved to be that for me. I was devastated by my first crush and I was sinking further with all the heaviness around me at home. It felt so cruel, not being able to chase it all away. It had a stickiness like honey and became too difficult to wash away without warmth and enough-ness. I needed that warmth and couldn't find it so the heaviness made a home in me.

Those days were brutal with those same catty girls and inappropriate boys making known their thoughts on my style, my body, my hair, and my choices in friends who were also not cool enough to be enough. It so happened that my particular lunch period was with none of my friends. Well my one friend anyway who was sparkly, sweet, a bit overweight by any popular standards, and a funny girl who could keep me laughing when I didn't believe the heaviness would allow it.

I could not fathom the idea of trying to locate a safe haven to eat in that was within the boundaries of the school campus. There was no place to escape the snickering, the commenting, or the terrified way I was sure I would react if they knew how small I felt inside. I finally located the only place that felt secure and safe and it happened to be the bathroom. Terribly enough, I remember eating my PB&J's in there just about every day. If I was quiet and invisible enough I could escape there without anyone wondering why I wasn't coming back out. They weren't interested in gossiping about me if they couldn't see me so I became an invisible bathroom lunch eater. I never did tell my parents about all those days eating in the dark. They were not to be trusted with my heart. How could I betray myself that way when it was the last whole part of me with a little light left?

I was protecting it from the Darkness at home while eating in the dark at school in hopes that I could try to control it from the inside. That sticky honey heaviness was easing itself inside, oozing into all the cracks and shadows, but these lunches in the bathroom kept me safe from it all consuming me. At least, that's what I believed back then. Eating in that dark middle school bathroom was the safest domain I had until I was within the sanctuary walls of my room, down that long beautiful hallway to freedom inside that brown house with its two watchful eyes.

Saturday Daze

With all the Darkness would also come small, waking dream moments. They would allow me a breath of air that wasn't heavy or toxic. I like to think back on these as 'polliwog hunting' moments. They were short, crisp, and clear moments of light and hope. It was because of these moments, I would sometimes wear rose colored glasses in an effort to reach for their goodness. These moments were a refreshment of sorts, but they were not long lasting and did not withstand the strength of the storms. Grey and gloomy, they came without warning and without time to think through an escape. A lot of the weekends felt like those storms. Saturdays in particular were drenched in the grey that would always turn to dark.

My dad was away on trips most every week at this point. The longer he was a pilot, the more time we spent living in the shadows. I would recall him packing and taking his leave from the brown house most Sunday evenings. I would inwardly voice my hollers of celebration that he was going to be gone for 4 days while outwardly expressing only the tolerated missing of him. We were all playing roles in a game of emotional hide and seek. He would return on Friday nights and spend the weekends at home where nobody's schedules or ideas were voiced. We were buried under the Darkness as soon as he arrived back home.

Saturday mornings, I would be awake hours before I knew he would be; purposefully to avoid everything I knew was possible with his presence back home. There was a lot that was possible: disappointment in how my mom chose to parent in his absence, frustration with my sister's actions or school performance that week, irritation at how I may have exacerbated the home life for Mom or my sister with my own feelings. There was an outright disregard for feelings of any kind other than delight in him and everything he worked to provide. Of course, there were also so many simpler reasons that the Darkness would come; crumbs in the sink, dining room chairs not pushed in, drinks spilled at the table, and bedrooms that did not meet his standards of military cleanliness.

He would wake sometime late morning, and I would hold my breath waiting for all his idiosyncrasies to begin. His presence was always big and loud, never to be missed by any of us. It would all begin with the running water of the faucet, a second flush of the toilet, the roar of his sneeze, the obnoxiously loud throat clearing, the opening of the double doors to his room, and another throat clearing followed by the clambering of his feet flip flopping down the stairs that would bring his existence into my visual space and a reality for the day ahead. He would make his way through the breakfast that was always prepared and waiting for him at the table.

Without fail, it would be present and thoughtfully laid out with a folded napkin, a plate, and a large spoon resting and waiting. It was sometimes one of my Saturday morning chores to prep his breakfast so it was ready the minute he was downstairs. He never verbally expected or demanded it and was outwardly grateful for the weekly display of servantry, but he never requested that we let him do it for himself nor did he do it for anyone else. Breakfast was always a bowl of Corn Flakes with an entire, well ripened, banana sliced on top, a grapefruit halved and salted, a glass of orange juice, and a cup of coffee for his post eating newspaper reading and continued throat clearing. He had nothing to do but awaken when well rested, to then be waited on by a loyal and lovely wife who claimed to always do all the things simply because she wanted to. I would believe that, except I knew and understood the childhood version of existing here and the fear of not living up to his standards.

I knew that Saturdays with Dad were an equation of mixed up math that never added up properly. We started with room cleaning which led to room cleaning again and sometimes a third time if inspection was not satisfactory. There were so many rules just for cleaning rooms that our mental lists were long and difficult to check off the first time. With no room for self-expression or individuality, our rooms were kept upwards of military cleanliness and expectation.

Every Saturday, it was never clean enough from the week before. Toys were not allowed out anywhere and only one treasure was allowed on our expertly made and inspected beds. We organized, we dusted, we vacuumed when we were allowed too, and we cleaned drawers, closets and bathrooms. If any drawer was missed or clothes not folded well enough, the contents were dumped to the floor until it was done right. I can remember one weekday I came home from school to find every drawer emptied of its contents and in piles on my floor. Mom had done that. The shadows were searching for her during the days at home now and every once in a while, she let them in and reacted in a way that the Darkness would just to keep it from coming so frequently. Every Saturday it was never clean enough from the week before. Every Saturday it was like starting over again and knowing that it was never good enough at the start or the finish.

Once room cleaning was done, it was time to start the yard work. He renamed it yard 'beautification' to make it sound lively and interesting and that may have been the only saving grace about it. The sun was warm on those Saturday yard days and we spent lots of time re-doing the work again since nothing could pass inspection it seemed. We used yard scissors to painstakingly trim the edging of the grass since we weren't allowed to use the edger that would have shortened the work considerably. We weeded until every single weed was removed and maybe even some that weren't really weeds at all.

It was difficult to see the difference sometimes. There was always room for improvement. I think as a child who was fragile at best, I needed to know that sometimes good enough was enough to be considered helpful and treasured too. Perfection reigned over our home from the inside out because the Darkness believed it to be necessary for value and worth. It had too in order to be a calming force for his own shadowy corners. He would speak as though that were not the case but then his actions would not correlate. It was that messed up terrible math problem. The one that just never added up.

He would continuously override a need within himself for a realization of who he was and how he could have been the Different we all needed him to want to be. In his own dark corners he would deny that need altogether because it would keep everyone else so aware of how difficult we made things. We could always be the ones to blame that way. He would effortlessly situate us in shadows that kept us needy and compliant. He would keep his own corners out of his sight line by placing us all in the way.

He refuses to this day to visit his Darkness, to allow his own wounds to heal. He allowed two young girls to work those Saturdays the way he demanded and until he felt it was all finished. What he didn't see was the disconnect he was promoting. Those two young girls were unaware at that time, that their own self-worth was already precious even if he hadn't first enforced the dusting, vacuuming, organizing, trimming, and weeding that he made them feel was needed for the Darkness to see them that way. Not just one time of earning worthiness, but every weekend. Every Saturday the work to be seen as precious and of worth would begin all over again and of course that messed up math problem never did add up to anything that made any sense at all.

Walking To and Fro

When Darkness was away and the sun brought its warmth, Mom and I would sometimes take walks. Long walks. Walks that would bring out truths that I could not possibly fathom or know where to compartmentalize. These long walks seemed to invite the Darkness in even when he was away. The pain and the unknown were alive while the sun was bright and we were breathing in that fresh air. I wanted it all to be left behind in that house, but the Darkness followed me now. I could no longer leave it in the dark corners where it laid waiting.

We would walk and she would talk and all the poison would seep out of her like a faucet turned on high and left forgotten. She spoke words claiming her knowledge of the Darkness soon after they were wed, but knew she was too young and too resistant to want to be reminded of a second wrong marriage. She had felt his wrath and knew it was existent in between their warmer newlywed moments. She told of how the Darkness had lashed out on me when I was a crying infant, a fate that I have always believed began his distaste for me. She was hurt and angry and the walls of their first home had closed in on her.

When she was angry and upset at his physical reaction to my crying, she was given a harsh ultimatum to stay or to go if she didn't like his way of doing things. It wasn't clear after his threat whether he had allowed his shadows to guide him that day, or she had just been too emotional over his angry response. She chose to stay. She had hoped for More too. When she stayed that day, she chose to live underneath the Darkness. She chose to take the risk of a future with an unpredictable man that she realized she hadn't known long enough before their wedding day.

She chose to walk with me. She chose to allow me to see. She chose to reveal all that I did not know. She made it known that she believed she should never have had a family with him in the Dark. She revealed that he was not capable of being a warm parent the way a child needed. The warm being I had been hoping for was never going to be possible.

She wanted to leave. She wanted to leave many times. She threatened it to me and my sister as though we would fight it and beg her not too. As though we were the only ones who could fill her with the sanity to leave or the courage to stay. I begged her more than once to leave him. I pleaded through tears for her to take us and just go. I was desperate for Light and fresh air and sometimes in desperation I prayed for him not to return those late Friday nights or for me to just not wake up. I pleaded with myself to just be better, to be a better example, a perfect example of the little girl he could always show love and affection. Darkness would probably be Light if I could do that. I blamed myself for the Darkness, for all of it. He seemed to always want me to after all. When I cried and he couldn't console or control me, I started the story of shadows and a Darkness that couldn't be controlled as a crying and inconsolable infant left in his care.

On those long walks, she would tell me that she wished she had never married him and she believed that within those few moments before and after their vows, she had chosen a dark story. On those walks, she allowed the Darkness to sink in further in a way that was detrimental to my well-being. Knowing more doesn't always provide empowerment. Knowing more about who the Darkness was when nothing could turn into Light, left me reeling, deeply afraid, and protective of what was left to hold on too. Whatever was left to cling to that allowed me to feel whole, became incredibly fragile.

My mother—I unwillingly became a protector of her soul, a confidant, and a listening ear. It was only later that I would understand this forced and unwanted role. This power position she handed to me, would create chaos and ultimately devour me. The air would become stale and fraught with heaviness the more time that passed. I know too many hidden truths now. I had heard her words of truth. I witnessed her fragility as it fought with her strength. Her dilemma was always going to be choosing between this life with two children and a husband that appears on the outside to be flourishing, and knowing that the right choice for the three of us would be to tear it all down. A forced kind of happiness only appears that way for so long before people see that you hide in the shadows.

When his Darkness had come, it arrived in bold flashy colors damaging the inside of our homes and us with traumatic force. Dad had done that without ever seeing that he had. He never saw what we did or felt the damage in his wake the way we breathed in that dark, heavy air. He was never responsible for his words, his actions, or his opinions and somehow he managed to live outside of his Darkness enough that he could paint pretty pictures that ironically only he could see. His pretty pictures within his hours of choosing the perfect greeting card for birthdays, and holidays. Their words that would make Mom cry as she read them aloud in front of us all even though every time the Darkness arrived, she was weary and paralyzed.

After some of his tirades, he would drag me along to jewelry stores, making me try on rings, necklaces, bracelets that he thought she would adore and appreciate and all the while I now knew what her deepest truths and real feelings were about him. She would open whatever he ended up picking out and more tears would fall. I watched with outrage, confusion, and a sickening hope. A combo of emotions that would begin creating the colors of a terribly mixed painter's palette. Colors that were all mixed up together with other colors, drab, and dull, so ridiculous they were without a name. Somehow within those magic and sad words on those greeting cards along with that expensive gift giving, all would be well. Until they weren't. Again and again, over and over it was like living out an endless loop that would just keep repeating.

The walks with Mom would repeat, the bitterness from her would grow, and as the secret threats would continue, so would his gift-giving attempts at keeping her hoping and wanting. Then one day, the pretending and denial began. The conversations on our walks changed. They became about how I needed to change, I needed to be different in my own views on Dad and the Darkness. The gaslighting words that it was of my own making. 'It could be worse' and 'This is just who he is, he's not going to change' became the new themes for those grey walks where the Darkness seemed to now carry shadows along within my mom's words.

When the fight is discouraged long enough, the fear is replaced with complacency. The Darkness could control her in that space of ignoring what is and pretending that it's actually not there at all. Maybe it never really was. I realized then that in order for my mom to live safely in the shadows, she had to rewrite the story and she needed me to do the same.

The Table

Dad always had the luxury of leaving until he could seemingly forget the story that he wrote in the dark. He wouldn't return home before believing a new narrative he would use to rewrite those dark moments we were left existing in and reeling from. I understand now that this was the only way he could face himself every day and believe that perfectionist persona he needed reflecting back at him every morning.

The family dining table served as the scene for a lot of these rewritten stories. It would be the staple through a lot of our moments with the Darkness. I am quite certain it had known the Darkness before we had since it belonged to him before my parents were married. It was a part of his past and maybe that table understood him in ways we would never be able to. Maybe the table had witnessed Darkness from before, darkness that hadn't even belonged to him but had begun its shaping in the shadows.

I remember hearing that family dinners at the table were the greatest way to maintain connection and have a delightful end of day conversation where everyone listens to each other's tales of joy or woe with shared happiness or concern. My recollection of family dinners was not that. My memories are of ridicule over school work not done well, different choices needing to be made with friends, corrections on table manners, waiting for cues to begin eating and asking for seconds, or simply waiting to be excused.

Managing to remember to put my hair up in a ponytail before each meal, as that was demanded, was anxiety ridden enough, let alone hoping that my sister and I would manage to make it through without spilling our glass of milk. The table was an heirloom piece from my dad's family and so, as with most museum-like things in our house that belonged to him, it wasn't really meant to be used, but we did anyway. It seemed it was more than just an old table. It seemed too often be a set up to fail, to keep us in place, to keep him the authority. A visual reminder that things were of more value than feelings.

Although it also housed numerous birthday meals, breakfasts before school, and that one terribly confusing evening where my dad showed up with makeup and jewelry on, it was also a representation of the shadows that the Darkness held within. I have never been able to fathom why we actually dined on it based on the rules with everything else he owned. Like his family's gold couch in the living room that was never to be sat on. Our only moment on that gold couch was Christmas morning which made every breath a prayer that we would manage to somehow not destroy it with our nervous energy.

The table had cracks in it where the hinges would allow for it to become an even bigger table with even bigger cracks. Those cracks were a fumbly-fingered child's worst enemy. Each glass of spilt milk was literally cried over while we watched the liquid enemy seeping into those cracks and onto the rug below. This ended any semblance of a pleasant dinner as we were scolded for our stupidity, asked to leave the table and go to our rooms. Shame was poured onto already infested self-doubt as we may have also been berated over other things and told that we weren't good enough before that fated spill had even taken place.

I could never understand how my dad had a table that he saw as far more precious than the family sitting around it every evening that he was home. There were no other options but to come to the table when called. No places to hide or be invisible until the meal was over. No magic ways to create fewer accidents, no motivational self-talk that could make us be more careful.

As we got older, there were also incredibly terrifying and trauma filled table experiences when the Darkness would come unannounced. They always involved hideous shouting, stomping feet, pounding fists, irate name calling towards me and my mother, sister flying to her room in fear or in shame or both, and then, the storm would simply end. The tirade would lessen and eventually the Darkness would just be gone again. I always knew that after the terror had passed, my dad would leave. He would physically leave the house and for hours at a time. Nobody knew where he would go or what he did when he escaped to reboot and change the narrative about who he was and what he had done.

I can remember standing still with fear in the kitchen, knowing when he was about to explode with his internalized rage His face became distorted and red, practically pulsating with anger. His fists would turn white knuckled and his voice would raise to volumes that should have warranted a concerned neighbor or two. His words would be evil and demonstrative, and he would turn them on my mother and then on me. His shameful Darkness would fall on all of us those nights. My mom, who would try to use her voice and speak at first, would then twist it all upside down inside her head and be silenced with his threats and jarring attacks. She would then be silent for what seemed like days after, not speaking to anyone.

My dad would eventually return home. Whether that was hours after or the next morning I was never certain. I had stowed away in my room or with my sister knowing my mom had curled up in her bed and into her cave of shame and shadows. He would make his way down the stairs the next morning, robe in place and flip flops smacking each stair on his way back to the table for his breakfast. I would know instantly that he had placed that dark tirade somewhere else, some tidy little box deep inside his own shadowed corners. This is where he kept all his Darkness so he would never have to see the damage in its wake because it simply never happened and whatever did happen was not something he would be blamed for. There were never apologies, and never a down on your knees type of begging for forgiveness. It was simply swept away with the tide while we were left reeling, shaken, and without an escape from the shock of it all.

Mom, in her silence, would stay hidden away and would leave us with him sometimes for days. If she did make an appearance, it was never for long and no words were spoken. The Darkness would play coy and the blame would become my mother's for her reactions. He would have moments after those events of pouring out sickening sweetness towards us while Mom was in her cave.

He would take us to get ice cream, or on a drive where he would say things like, "Oh, you know, your mother gets this way if things aren't going the way she likes them." That was typically followed with, "I don't know how to explain your mother's behavior."

Between my dad and my mom, the insanity of it all went from crazed one moment to living within the emotional aftermath of the abuse the next.

And so it went, dinner at the table. An antique nightmare of an object for eating, and chaos creating, it was a place for anxiously anticipating a circus of unknowns and we were just waiting for what shadows would unveil themselves and what show was going to begin next. I honestly have no idea how I survived the years of meals there really. I have no recollection of goodness when I sat in my same chair with my same ponytail because now, all those moments that might have been wonderful and good, carry a heaviness now as I look back. I see how they have been jaded by those visits from the Darkness and the nightly anxiety of its impending return.

Practice Makes Perfect

The gold couch and its reign in our museum-like living room had been part of all our homes and would make the move to the next one as well. It would not see its last day until much later on when the Darkness was left with nothing except its shadows and had to make some concessions to move on. For now though, it stays in the background of this particular memory, taunting me every day that I had to walk into that off-limits room.

The only time I was ever able to spend more than Christmas morning in the gold couch room was when piano lessons became a part of my life. I know the kind of kid I was. I was lacking in determination and feared everything. I never knew how to be perfect enough to create any value for the Darkness so it became easiest to do only what I had to do and try to survive that. Until the day that my dad bought a piano. He had dabbled in it as a kid and wanted to continue to pursue it. He felt that if he were to take lessons, I should too. Lessons came with practice and practice came with lots of rules. There were so many rules for everything and now this too.

Practice was expected for an hour every day and practice on a song was meant to be repeated until it was done without mistake. The piano was not to be touched or approached without careful hand washing, a towel on the fabric bench seat, and a ponytail in place. We were not allowed to touch our face during practice or we would need to go wash our hands again. Once again, the unspoken words always seemed to be, 'nice things are valued more than people, and children should learn to live inside their environment versus the environment being safe for them to explore and grow within'. If Darkness was home during practice sessions, the rules were double-checked and the actual beauty of playing lost its luster.

When he was away, I wore my hair down. I played and wrote my own music and sometimes wrote lyrics too. I would still place the towel down and wash my hands first, hoping that it was enough to still be mindful while allowing a bit of myself out in the open. Eventually, the pleasure of stroking the keys and hitting the notes was betrayed by the need to be something, anything, which would be seen as okay enough for the Darkness.

With that being incredibly daunting, I eventually quit piano but he would still play sometimes. He would play the same songs over and over and over and we all had to make sure we told him how wonderful it sounded. Even though, he took some lessons too, he only ever played what he knew by heart. Every stroke of the keys was played as loudly as possible. Nobody was to miss hearing him do much of anything. Much like everything else, he needed to be praised an overwhelming number of times. Mom had to make sure and stroke his ego when asked and my sister and I were old enough now to know it was wise to follow suit. We were called out to see the cars when he was finished washing and waxing them all, he took us all out to the yard after he had fixed all our mistakes so we could see how it was supposed to look. So of course, the piano playing was to be acknowledged as well.

He did play well, he did everything well, but that was never the point. To do well and all of the time, was to be noticed and praised. Those shadow days when the Darkness would come, were different. They were not to be remembered or acknowledged at all. Those were never collected and tallied. He didn't see them, he erased them. We didn't discuss them, we didn't ask for clarification or understanding why. We were simply left shaking from them. We somehow knew he wasn't capable of any of that without delegating shame like it was his honor and right to do so. If we had made known that our insides felt like battle-laden war zones, he would be sure to negate any ownership. We would be left covering up more wounds that we simply had no extra room for.

We made sure that each day he was built up and given his pats on the back. "You played that song so well Dad," "The yard looks good Dad," "the car looks really nice and shiny Dad." He would in turn make sure we also saw how the counters in the kitchen shined after he cleaned up and that the carpet in the museum room had fresh vacuumed lines. He needed high fives and nice jobs any day he was home and when he had opportunities to give them out, the Darkness took over and he seemed to want to deal out shame while pointing out imperfections he saw instead.

He knew how to mold his household. He was in charge of a wife and two daughters and they were going to understand that their place was to live in the spaces of how he perceived us. We were to ride along on his whimsical drives to places he wanted to go, to do the things he wanted, listen to his music, strive for his perfection for approval, to not be emotionally needy, and to make sure he was lifted up high enough that we were left trembling with uncertainty of his behavior if we didn't play the game. We played by his rules. He was running his family just the way he thought he ought too, believing he was doing his best, and he was king.

The Christmas Kitten

She was a sweet bundle of cuteness and although we talked about other names, Dad named her all on his own. She was the Christmas kitten I had written Santa about with my sister's help and we were desperate for her. She was also a glimmer of hope in an otherwise fairly uncertain and unsafe existence. I have no idea how my dad agreed to an animal in our house. The light left within my mom must have begged, almost on her knees, for him to relent and say yes to the plea of her girls in the form of a letter to Santa.

In desperation for something real and tangible, and compelled to want to believe my parents would do the inconceivable, I wrote the letter. It worked, and somehow the Light intercepted the Darkness long enough to leave us at home for an entire day while they made a secret journey out together to bring the kitten home. She was beautiful and soft, warm and real. She was simply the most wonderful treasure we had been given. At first all was well. There were lots of rules, of course, and chores for kitty care were handed out readily. She was playful and fun and so tiny. It is difficult, as one can imagine, to have pets in your home and not assume that things might get messy on occasion and at times, rules will be broken.

Once Dad discovered that control was not entirely his with a tiny kitten around, everything changed. She discovered places to hide, she coughed up fur balls, she made a litter box trail, and she wasn't always cooperative when it came to grooming. The worst of it was the day she discovered the museum-like living room and the gold couch. The Darkness came and was more than angry. I remember the physical reaction to his realization that she was perched on the back of that couch. I saw her before he did but simply couldn't get to her in time.

It came quickly and without warning like it usually did. The stomping and clapping, the yelling and screaming at her to get off and get out. His angry and distorted face, the one he wore at 'the table', terrified us all and now terrified the cat too. She was angry in return and left the room in a hurry, hissing and talking back. From that day on, if she was in that room or anywhere else she didn't belong, she was squirted in the face with water and chased through the house while he spat out words and stomped at her. She became an unfriendly, fearful, not-playful kitten who took to hiding most of the day under beds. She knew the Darkness now too and it was changing her like it had changed us. It slowly started turning out all the lights.

My joy of that beautiful gift melted away like everything good and joyful seemed too. She had been so tiny and dependent on affection to keep her wanting to be near us. She had been unaffected by the past that we had lived, but now she knew to hide away in secret sanctuaries too. With all of my memories and dark moments with my dad, I remember being so angry at him for so very long over this. Angry because he would never see his own dark shadows. To this day, he never remembers their appearances or the stench of fear that he would leave after each fitful episode. He never could understand why Fluffy didn't like him. He took personal offense to her dislike of him after that. He couldn't seem to make sense of it and hated her immensely for it. She became just another victim that was brought into our home without knowledge of the reality of what lived there or the ability to choose to stay.

I loved her. I needed her, but I never should have written that letter and asked for her. She lived under the bed most days he was home after that. She was scared of the Dark. Ironically, her story with my dad ended 16 years later in a different house long after my sister and I had left. She came out from under the bed. Dad had finally stopped chasing her. She found his lap one day instead of the bed. She stayed there until she passed away and he tearfully let her go. He was so in love with her at the end and she seemed to love him too. He never wanted her and yet in the end he was the only one who ended up with her attention. Maybe she knew something we still don't know. Maybe she saw his shadowed corners and understood. Maybe he couldn't hide them from her like she hid under the bed. Maybe somehow she was okay with all his broken pieces. Maybe she just knew he needed her, perhaps the most out of all of us from the very beginning.

Writing that letter began a story that I couldn't have predicted the end too. I only wish I would have known her as the sweet and loving cat that she ended up being. I only wish I could have saved her from the Darkness that day before she knew a life of fearing it. I only wish that I knew what she began to understand about Dad. The way she eventually softened him, and warmed him. Almost the same way Grandma had.

Dark Hours

The nights were a paradox of sanctuary and sadness. The quiet was necessary, but the night was also lonely. I remember many nights going to bed feeling alone with my uncertain and unpredictable thoughts. My heart was attempting to place them all in a box that I would learn to sort through when I understood what I was feeling. I remember being soothed to slumber by the sound of the shower running on those nights where Dad needed to be ready to leave early in the morning. I don't know if it was the water that soothed me or knowing that it meant that when I woke, he would be away. He would be gone and the Light was able to find cracks to shine through and warm me up. I was so cold inside. Frigid to the bone. Desperate enough for a warmth that would fill me up and stay without strings attached. But the fear of knowing that wasn't real left me shaking and parched. I was reaching for it in those dark nights, being soothed by the water until sleep took me under.

From those junior high years and on, I remember asking many times to fall asleep and never wake up. Never to wake anymore to the breathless unknown every day. The walking into each day with hope and fear in how they would begin and end was breaking me. There was nowhere to store up all of the emotions I wasn't given any space to feel. There was not enough time each day to reach the perfection that was asked for and be good enough. There was fear to wrestle with, uncertainty to escape, and people to protect. The daily journey of needing to be who he wanted out of expectation while also learning how to just be me, was too much. I couldn't do it anymore. There was too much hard and too much hurt. Home was not a sanctuary and family was not safe.

It is such an intense existence to be in when you are forced to exist within the reality of choices your parents decided to live out as their own twisted versions of truth. They believed with certainty that their version of the best they could do as parents was avoiding the reality of what was, not seeking out guidance, and asking my sister and I to pay the emotional price for it. Their version of the best was not the best at all. It was never going to be. Their version of the best they could do was avoiding the reality of what we were living in, not seeking guidance for a tool box of choices in better parenting and a better marriage, and asking my sister and I to carry the shame of it all.

Their decisions led to a lifetime of heart wrenching healing for us both. We are still deep in the process of healing from our childhood trauma. We may always be in those trenches. Sometimes it may look and feel like we have climbed out and are walking above it all. Those moments of upward movement are walked carefully atop fragile tightropes along jagged edges of cliffs. It is difficult and intense work. It means carefully living within the fragility of being clipped in on that mountain and maintaining forward movement to avoid a triggering event that leaves you free falling into trenches of recovery and processing. It is not something I ever thought I would still be working through in my 40s. But here we are.

Those dark hours in the night were where it all began; the growing, the changing, the shifting in my knowledge that this was not okay. None of it was. The Darkness was spreading; seeping into my veins and devouring my bloodstream. Hope for More and Different was failing me. Thank goodness I was made stronger than I ever knew. Thank goodness I was able to withstand its attempts to control all of me. The challenges would continue and the Darkness would stay on a destructive path, but the warmth was a temptress. The warmth always found a crack to seep into. Those nights of sanctuary and sadness let in just enough warmth. Just enough warmth to quiet the voice that was hoping not to wake up.

T.P. and Bird Face

His name was Matt and he lived down the street. He was loud and obnoxious, a bully and a creator of chaos. He was an average looking teenage boy with pimples, a long, lanky body, and a bad attitude. Most days he would see me in the neighborhood on my bike or walking with my sister to our friend's house down the street. I would choose to ignore him, he would choose to call me names. He would refer to me as 'bird face' because he probably was all too familiar with this type of behavior at home. There seemed to be a limitless list of reasons that allowed boys to get away with bad choices and a self-righteous chip on their shoulder. He became my worst nightmare for one summer season and one night in particular, he woke the Darkness.

It was a terribly chilly Friday night and Dad was home. I was already asleep when he barged into my room without warning. He loomed over my bed, enraged and spitting words that shook me awake and sent my heart racing. Our house had been egged and toilet-papered, it needed to be cleaned up immediately, and it was my fault. It was my fault because if I wasn't always 'prancing through the neighborhood', boys wouldn't notice and make bad decisions. It was my fault for being seen. It was my fault for existing and that a dumb teenage boy with pimples and a bad attitude who called me names, had noticed.

The Darkness made me get out of bed, get dressed, and clean it all up in the middle of the night. The toilet paper wasn't strung in the trees or thrown on the house, it was shredded in tiny pieces all over the front lawn and the sprinklers had just shut off. It was torn up, soaking wet, difficult to see in the dark and painstaking to clean up in the chilly early morning hours. While Dad attempted to clean the egg off the front door and mailbox, I was in the grass on my hands and knees shivering and covered in the shame of what I had allowed to happen while also not really understanding how I could have prevented it.

It didn't matter if I could have. The Darkness found ways to play with the chaos within and the shame was always there tumbling around inside my panic and desperation to make it all go away. If it wasn't this, it would have been something else. Bent over in the damp and cold I was greeting the weekend through tears and fear. I knew how Saturdays were spent. I was just getting a head start.

The next morning, my shame was on display. My mom knew, my sister knew and the tension over what I had caused was palpable. My mom may have wanted to intervene on my behalf but knew what tangible anger she would rile up if she did. So, she didn't. My dad hadn't calmed down and the Dark display continued. He demanded I go with him to the terrible boy's house to confront him and his parents and demand an apology. We didn't get one of course. The chaos creator, that boy named Matt, didn't admit to anything. Instead, his mother alarmingly suggested that 'Boys will be boys' and that was that. My dad said words that I can't remember in my devastation of having to stand there facing this boy like I was the criminal. I never knew for sure that this boy was the culprit, but I remember his face behind his mother at the door looking at me with almost empathy. He didn't know who my dad was. He couldn't have known what he would wake up in his efforts to be a bully. He almost seemed sad about it. Dad continued to berate me for the mess on the heavy walk home. Irony doesn't play fair.

After that, the boy named Matt never called me Bird Face again. He became quieter when he passed my house and just watched in silence if he saw me around. Maybe that alone accounted for his guilt or maybe he recognized something familiar that he now knew lived in my house to something that lived in his. What I know for certain, is that the Darkness continued to show me that Dad was never in my corner. He was fighting for a perfection that would never exist inside and out and when he didn't' get it, he would send everyone into shadowed corners filled with shame, self-deprecation, and a terrifying determination to please him hoping it would all just go away. We would have done anything to keep the Darkness quiet and still. I longed for those Polliwog hunting days and I hoped they were as light and warm as I remembered them.

The Announcement

It was a Sunday. The Camero was breezy and warm from the sun as it poked in through the open top on the way home. I remember sitting down for lunch around 'the table' and taking a few moments to hope for a drama free experience as I had gotten in the habit of doing. I knew when the mood shifted; I could sense the Darkness waiting in the periphery. I was weeks away from the end of my junior year in a very small high school that had taken me away from the bullying and the ridicule of earlier years. There I was gloriously involved in carefree everyday things that kept me away from the fight or flight of home base. I could not imagine why the Darkness wanted to rear itself now.

The Darkness, perhaps it tired of peering in from the outside of things, made a grand entrance that Sunday at 'the table'. My dad announced that we would be moving and not just around the corner, or to a new neighborhood nearby. We were leaving California altogether and heading to Washington State to begin what he referred to as his reach for retirement.

It was more than a shock. I was immediately taken to a place of no air, no breath, and completely reeling in the reality of what this all meant. I begged them to allow me to stay behind, to have my senior year with the friends who had done nothing short of saving me. My parents didn't know how lonely I had been, how lost I had felt, and how I had asked to be taken away from the confusion and heartache nightly and for months. In tears, I begged almost to my knees. They wouldn't listen to any of my requests, my pleadings, or any of my friends' families inviting me to stay with them and finish school. I would have done anything to be free and happy, without the shadows that were always there, waiting for his Darkness to play us like puppets on strings.

I was silenced. I wasn't allowed to talk about how this decision was affecting me. After a while, I couldn't speak at all. I couldn't think of anything to say that wouldn't unleash my insides. To not tell the truth of how I was achy all the time. How my lungs cried out in silence with no one to hear. How my confidence was based on the pettiness of being pretty because Dad would only compliment me if I was. How I never stopped wishing that Mom would leave him to save the last bits of us that were left so he couldn't destroy them too. It all would have escaped my lips if I had let it. I would have been punished and reminded of how all of those things were nobody's fault but my own. So I stayed silent.

There was nothing to be done. I had to turn into a shell of myself to become what my parents were asking me to be to make this move and do it without being rude, unhappy, or emotionally needy. I had to learn to acknowledge my gratitude over anything they were allowing me to do before we left for good. There was no hand holding, no check-ins, no room for a disappointed, angry, and very scared me.

I was leaving everything. All the people, places and things that had become my resting place so I could be free when I wasn't at home in my room. It all seemed so unreal, so cruel, and my insides were splitting in two. The irony of what would eventually happen to our family is the saddest part of the whole story. The Darkness was not staying within old memories, and 'the table' and the gold couch came along for the next chapter too.

Part 3
Creating the End

A Prelude to Madness

The new house in a new state was white. A color of innocence, and the unknown. A seemingly clean slate. Maybe no more brown house meant no more brown statues, no more dinner table nightmares, no more shadows lurking when we began to loosen our hold on our fear of the Dark. Maybe it never mattered what color the houses were. The Darkness was living among us and nothing as trivial as a color would change that.

It goes without saying that we needed counseling. I needed counseling. We needed help out of the forsaken and dark-laden waters we had learned to tread in just enough to keep our heads from going under. We needed someone to grab hold, fish us out, and hold on. Keeping us from the need to jump back in for fear of the outside being even colder with reminders of all our shame. We were supposed to feel lucky. We were supposed to be grateful. We had a home to live in, two parents, enough food to eat, and clothes to wear.

What becomes of a person with so many wounds open and laying exposed beneath the surface of the murky dark waters. After so long breathing underneath it, inside the tyranny and the abuse, it seemed like we had created the Darkness ourselves. How do you ask for help when you believe it's your own fault that you're trying not to drown? Getting help was never something that was referred to, talked about, or considered. The Darkness didn't want to give up his control or be asked to question his actions. After I left, I heard about attempts made at help for my sister's sake, but nothing healing seemed to last and nothing changed. Dad would always leave when it seemed like help was asking him to own what he had done and uncover the why of it all.

I want to acknowledge that today, I am okay. I am living with a healing heart, and with a nurturing husband who sees all of it. He knows the stories of the Darkness and saw a lot of it himself. I have known for many years now that the Darkness I lived with was a deeply rooted trauma. Childhood trauma filled with verbal, emotional, and at times physical abuse. I have received years of counseling that I sought out for myself. I knew that I needed it when I chose to be a mom in my own right and begin my own family. I knew that I wanted a different path and to reach for a cleansed spirit for my own journey of family. I knew I needed and wanted to break the cycle of trauma for my family.

The growing and the healing and the reaching into the furthest shadowed corners of my story has been beyond difficult. I won't muddy it, simplify it, and say it has been a quick fix or a straight path. It has taken years of digging, sifting, managing emotions, and learning to claim them without being ashamed of them all. It has been endless and will continue to be. I am thankful for wise counsel and my own family who is aware of who I am and what I grew up in. A family who also knows I adore all their parts and facets of self.

We live in the knowledge of truth together and our girls have never known my dad the way I did. They have never known the Darkness and we have protected them from it when we felt its presence lurking in the shadows. The Light of awareness and healing is full of surprises and it has gifted me with lifelong healing and the ability to see and live outside the murkiness of the shadows.

It may seem that therapy should have been obvious to all of us as we got older, but when you are living in and experiencing trauma, you just ache to survive it. That Darkness is not recognized for what it is. Many don't choose to recognize emotional abuse as actual abuse which in turn renders the victim helpless and wanting to leave what is seen as stability in a nurturing home by anyone looking in from the outside. It can't be seen for what it is until you are existing and taking breaths outside of it. I read recently that it takes abuse victims, typically women, seven attempts on the average, to leave their abuser, for good. They return to what they have always known, over and over and over.

The Darkness repeats its tirades, they try again to leave, but the shadows dance around inside creating chaos and worthlessness until they return, again and again and again. To live on the other side of all pretty homes with playful backyards, brown houses with watching eyes, and whitewashed ones with no memories, takes seven tries. Not knowing how to feel worthy, capable, and free enough to live without what has always been known as their stability, keeps them where they are. This is all part of the control and manipulation of the abuser's cycle.

The Dark stays with you, anywhere you are, taking root inside your veins. Your strength can grow and your inner light is there, but it remains hidden away until you are able to leave for good. Until you uncover where it is hidden, nourish it with goodness, and provide it with the knowledge it needs to ignite.

The mixed abuse trauma that we experienced in our family is a fluid memory because of the shame and responsibility I felt for it. Did it happen? Was it really my experience? Were those terrifying moments as scary as I recalled them? The Darkness would fool me into believing more than once, that they never took place. Even years later when I approached my dad and asked him he couldn't recall any of it. Couldn't believe he could have said those things or acted that way. That's what all the leaving after the Darkness expelled itself provided him. He could leave it and then deny it and become that well liked, white-washed version of himself.

Years later, I asked him to listen. I asked him to validate my memories and the damage they had left behind. He denied many of them and didn't offer any apologies but instead claiming he had always done the best he knew to do. After all, he would say, there is no guidebook for parenting.

My mother continued her threats of leaving, always verbal to only us, and attempted to leave my dad multiple times, if only just in thought. She managed to come close one weekend, but in the end, she didn't. She didn't leave him until one winter, for 6 months, and many years later.

Around the time I started writing this book, she left. It was a tumultuous time and I was left picking up the pieces of them both for those long months. While walking Mom, shaking and teary, through the first several weeks, she began counseling on her own. Dad would call every day sobbing about his mistakes in the Dark, the ones he had made with her. She needed my strength, as she always had, and now Dad needed my sympathy. He was broken, and blaming himself in a way I had never known him to do. He was lost without her. Of course he was.

Even after so many years, I was roped right back into the trauma cycle of hoping and having that hope fade. She went back. After six months of picking herself up and living in a space of her own making where she could thrive, she went back. He made promises and she believed them all. Some were small and some were going to take more effort. He remains good at the small promises, but the bigger ones were too difficult to pursue and she decided she was okay with that.

They remain together to this day and not far from me and my own family, where we moved all those years ago into that innocent white house. They live in their own kind of bubble now. They have walked many paths since all of these stories took place and I think they believe that the Darkness isn't with them anymore. They attempted therapy together again upon my mother's insistence after she moved back home. For reasons they gave that seemed more like excuses, they stopped. The attempt wasn't the first, but they always ended the same way.

It was too hard for him, things may have happened because of him and he couldn't fathom the reasons to blame himself. She had insisted on the help they needed to open up wounds that were triggers. She had insisted, but as soon as things felt okay enough, he was being helpful enough, and he moved into a smaller home that she insisted on, she just agreed to stop the help. Again. I have my thoughts on why, but at the end of the day, this is their story now. Not mine. They live in a carefully crafted bubble of denial that the Darkness is gone. Maybe it is, or maybe it's just hovering above the surface of those murky waters.

I am saddened to think that shadows still dance around Mom. I lost count of the number of times she would threaten to leave, but I am certain she will never leave again. She will never reach her seven and now she doesn't speak to me of the Dark anymore. I have asked her not to. It is devastating that any woman has to fathom how to leave, how to ask for help, or to carry her children through that kind of trauma. Once removed from it, the work becomes how to provide for them all while hiding from their abuser and being dependent on a broken system to help them do it.

It's not hard to reason why my mother never left when we were young. I can remember vividly her telling me that if she left him, she would be terrified of his temper and how difficult he would make our life when the Darkness came. She was stuck and knew she was controlled by it. She was controlled by her position as a stay at home Mom and all the resources came from him. Her desperation for a life with few financial concerns kept her in place, treading water and waiting. She would make the meals, clean the house, and buy the groceries. She would do it all to keep him aware of her value in hopes that the Darkness would stay away. It never mattered how much she did. Please don't take seven tries. You deserve the warmth without the chill of the shadows, without the dark luring you back inside on repeat.

The Car

The thing about abuse is that many times, it lays dormant. Maybe only for days, sometimes weeks, or maybe even months. You know that it's there and you tiptoe around it like it were a quietly hibernating bear on the floor that lies in every room you walk through in every effort to leave it sleeping. It felt initially like starting over in this innocent white house. Like all the Darkness had been left in California; in the walls and the floors of our other homes and left for new families to find. Some time went by but it only took some living and circumstance for the shadows to find us.

After our move, I remained quiet. I felt like I hadn't really spoken much at all since their announcement, at least not when I was home. It was understood that if I was around my parents, I was to show only happiness and appreciation. Negative emotions were denounced and punishment handed out with anything they could make an impact with. I did all I could to comply with their wishes and live in the heaviness of having to leave what had felt like goodness and light to me. The move felt like a punishment in and of itself. I could feel in my bones that the longer we were in this new home, in this new place, the Darkness was approaching. I was aware that I was still being silenced for feeling negatively about the move, but I knew that not complying would always lead to a more controlled environment.

Eventually, after months of riding the bus to a new school, I was able to find a job to pay for my gas money so I could drive myself like I used to. The car was one that my dad had purchased for me before my 16th birthday. Looking in from the outside, it seemed wonderful, like our family often was perceived, and also made me look utterly spoiled. The expectation from us for any outwardly wonderful thing that Dad did was an extensive amount of gratitude. Over and over, we audibly had to note how wonderful it was that he was so generous.

On the inside, I wanted it all to disappear. These were not gifts, they were extended ways to keep us living like those puppets. To keep us wanting, to keep us needing from him, and to keep us in line. This car that I needed in order to also do what was expected was a new source of anxiety. From the moment I would arrive home, Dad would immediately come and 'inspect' the car. He made me walk around the car with him, slowly and with intention, looking for faults; scratches from carelessly unlocking the door with the key, dents from poor parking jobs, roughed up tires from hitting a curb, or gas streaks after a lazy fill. Driving was stress inducing. It came with many car inspections accompanied by shame placing and blame focused commentary if anything was discovered.

The crash happened one midafternoon on my way to work. I sensed it before I felt it. I had a moment of knowing, of feeling as though I was flying out of my own body. The car struck the driver's side, spinning me out of the intersection and stopping me facing 90 degrees from where I had been. My airbag opened and my seatbelt squeezed where it needed to. The older man who hit me had turned left on a red light. The good news was that he was okay and it wasn't my fault. Not technically speaking anyway. I remember having no concern for the shape I was in, as long as it wasn't my fault.

He was on a trip that week. Where he was, I don't remember; I only recall being grateful he wasn't going to be home when I got there. I refused a ride to the hospital and Mom came to take me home. I have no recollection of where the car went at that point. I know that in the end, it was not salvageable but, soon after, along came another car that I didn't want.

My clearest memory of this particular evening was the phone call from Dad when he learned what had happened. He didn't ask me if I was okay, although he probably already knew that. He didn't wonder how I had felt in the moment, he didn't ask if I was scared. He wanted to know how the damage to the car was. He wanted to know if I had caused the accident, if it happened because of anything I had done. Once he knew that it wasn't, I don't remember talking about it again. I had whiplash, painfully bruised ribs, injuries from the seatbelt, was scared shitless and couldn't talk about it. My mom was upset at me even though she was concerned for me. It was just another moment caused by me for her to be afraid of the Dark. Afraid of the aftermath from his possible rage and disappointment.

Living in the dark means fighting every day to get to the surface where you can see that the light is ablaze. We never found our way there together as a family. Sister and I are paving our way through the healing, slowly walking through all the ramifications of surviving in Darkness for so long. Like touring a museum of history with all of its shocking truths and sordid stories. The way through the mucky waters of shame and loss of light is daunting, but it is not without rewards.

But on that day, in that world in the dark, I couldn't see past it all. The shame of the accident was another scar, another shadowed corner. I still couldn't speak to them about this move, the massive size of this new school and the clique-ness of the kids. The ugliness of it all was growing every day. The cat had found new hiding spots. I wanted to hide away every day too, just to keep it all away under the murky water.

Winter Out the Window

It was so bright. I had never seen snow, never touched it, and never watched it falling from my bedroom window. I saw lots of it that first Christmas in the new white house, all from the vantage point of my new safe space.

I don't have any memory of what caused the disdain and shadowed holiday that winter. It might have been me wanting to spend time with the new boy who had crossed my path and invited me to spend the day with his family. It might have been my sister who had already been in trouble with the new friends she was making. It might have been my parents who hadn't seemed happy since the move that late August day.

One Christmas in the brown house with the watching eyes, I remember my dad being upset about something when he put up the tree and the rest of the day we kept separated just to keep the Darkness at bay. This day felt a lot like that one. There were gifts under the tree, the new living room sparkled with the holiday and though we weren't allowed to step foot in it on a regular day, today was the day we should be sitting in there. It was vacuumed perfectly with the carpet lines in place. It was dusted, polished, and the gold couch shimmered from no use.

The piano was there too. He still played his same song without fail, over and over until it was just right. The living room had always just existed. It had just been a room that occupied space and looked perfect; in the brown house, and now the new white house. It was Christmas though, and we weren't in that room or sitting on that gold couch. Even through the knowing that we would worry about what we wore, or what we had on our skin that might leave an oily stain, I would have given anything to have had a 'normal' day and been in that museum room, sitting on that terrible couch that would tempt the shadows away from their hiding places. We had unknowingly lured them out anyway, just by being.

I knew that in order to exist that day, and not fall completely apart with the somber mood, I had to stay in my room. Sister and I did what we could to celebrate and it seemed as though my parents preferred that we were in there anyway. We wore our holiday headbands and listened to Christmas music. We tried to giggle about things that didn't really matter. We silently reassured each other that we weren't as terrible as we were often made to feel, that we were enough, and watched the snow fall out the window. We watched it get deeper and heavier and it reminded me of how being here felt. Deeper into the murky dark water and somehow even heavier than what we had left behind.

I knew we hadn't really left it behind. It was here, it was haunting us like a ghost. The shadows and the dark knew how to find us no matter where we went now. The day turned into night and we knew we had escaped it. That Christmas Day we spent alone, in a new place, in the new white house, and new white weather, but at least we had been separated from the Darkness for a while.

I don't remember how the day ended, I don't remember opening gifts, or enjoying cider and listening to music like we normally did. I think that in order to exist within this controlled and emotionally upending environment, in order to survive a parent who was unaware of how he was imparting his undiagnosed issues on us all, Christmas that year was just a day that I watched from my window and the heavy snow was a metaphor.

About the Boy

There was a boy. He wasn't a toilet paper torturer or a dog poop trickster. He was a light bearer. The night we met was out of a storybook, a narrative not written for someone like me. It was not meant for the story I was living. That night was about another girl. A girl who had a different family from mine. She must have had a family who was strong, had honest laughter that wasn't masking deep pain; the kind that was real and inviting of the light. This girl had been given strength and she owned it, was proud of it. This girl had been allowed moments of failure without the following of the shame shadows. This wasn't supposed to be my story. It was futile to feel happy and dangerous to show it. Thrilling was the possibility of something real and light filled standing right in front of me.

We met at a youth group. I took myself there in one of the most courageous moments I had ever had. I was close to18 at this point and hoping for connection after the move. I had left all of that months ago and had been incredibly on my own navigating a new school and was tip-toeing around well-established groups of friends and keeping myself quiet around those who felt threatening. I was simply hovering above the ground not wanting my feet to touch this new space and hoping the year would be over soon.

He saw me first when I didn't even realize he was in the room. I walked into this space filled with new faces all directed towards me. I wanted to leave. This didn't feel like the warmth I had come from in my safe space and was desperately missing. He had a seat free next to him and offered it to me along with a cookie. For 5 years, he would offer me a space next to him and for most of those 5 years I took it. We had a difficult and beautiful relationship during that time. The darkness prevailed over many moments of it and for a while, I believed it would consume all the good that was there.

We became 'us' once we were strong enough to overthrow the shadows and break free of the hold the Darkness had on us for so long. We have learned and grown together and have raised two daughters for the past 25 years. We have a much different relationship with Dad now. There is light here and it shines bright most of the time. There are stories. Lots of them. We have lived through crazy bouts of dark and lonely; together and apart. Together we had a battle to fight for our own light and for our own story outside of all the shadows. He has always continued to offer me space to heal, to grow, to just be. He has always been a light bearer and he came just when my story knew I needed him to show up. He was the first person in my life since Grandma who wasn't afraid of the Darkness.

That One Summer

When high school was over, I had wanted things. I had wanted things that were my very own, that I held close to me and protected from the Dark. But all that was before the announcement of the move. Afterwards, those things vanished completely and I was left feeling empty. Nothing was clear or planned out in my head anymore. Darkness had been present as the days had passed after that first Christmas through the window and in some ways, more powerful and more shadowed than before.

My sister had not been magically transformed from her need for deep emotional crevices to be filled by things. We both needed those crevices to be healed, we just seemed to be looking for it in our own ways. The shadows knew that. They enjoyed creating chaos that the Darkness would use to plague us all.

The boy I met that one fateful night never seemed afraid, bullied away, shaken by the things he learned about the shadows I lived in, or how the Darkness would come and go. Our relationship took a toll on us both for lengths of time because of it however. In high school, the control over our time together complicated our first attempts at dating. This boy was different though, he was strong. There had been one boy before who was not. The timing for the two of us had never been right and the Darkness had never allowed that to become anything more than a tragic heartbreak between my dad's control and the boy's fears of it.

I couldn't blame him, of course. I watched him drive away from my house on our one and only date knowing that I had loved him as much I knew how too then and also knew he would never come back. My heart had known that likelihood all along, but the wishing had gotten in the way of the knowing and my heart had broken a second time that day because of it.

This boy though, he saw through all of it, and of all that he did see; he didn't run, never went silent, and persisted throughout the story. He was a hero to me in many ways and is still the most wonderfully human of beings that I have ever known.

When the knowledge grew within Dad that his control over our blooming relationship was not going to last, the Darkness became irate and grabbed at anything he could to take hold again. I was given ultimatums over financial support for future schooling and would have to leave the house if I didn't comply. What had been emotional and physical abuse trauma as a child was now morphing itself into a fierce control over my decisions and life choices.

We broke up twice during college due to threats and desperate grabs at control, but the first time was the most traumatic. College plans changed overnight and instead of continuing the trajectory I was on, my parents decided I would transfer a year early, sending me away to a school that was not the one my 'after the move' plan had intended.

Another rash decision was made to control my movements and my story.

The drop-off for that summer school semester left me reeling. I was again taken from a new community I was building and Darkness was leaving me somewhere new within shadowed walls, again. The decisions made were to keep him and I apart so that our time together was tethered. I felt alone, isolated, and confused as to what I had done or how I had behaved to warrant being dumped into newness all over again. There was no warm welcome, no decorating the dorm I was in, it was simply a quick, and impulsive move.

This seemed to be the pattern of the Darkness; creating waves and upheaval, leaving everyone in his wake repairing all the damage, alone. We didn't know how to survive it together. We were all left with our own feelings, our own guilt, and our own shame. We all had our own ways of locking away the pain. We didn't have the tools not to. He was a silencer and a bully, and as he seemed to enjoy it, he also didn't seem to know it. The confusion and the trauma always came when your guard was down and I always seemed to lessen the hold on mine.

I hadn't been guarding myself and now, I was standing in a strange new space, making a new bed, sharing a bathroom with a stranger, and putting on a smile when my parents left me there because I was afraid not to. What else would the Darkness have done if I hadn't? He had always threatened boarding school when we were younger if we misbehaved. I had mis-stepped, I had taken my own life into my own hands and made my own choices. The Darkness had sent me away because of it.

It took me weeks to establish another new rhythm and to convince myself again that I was going to be okay. The boy visited me in secret that summer. The shadows dissipated, and I was never more sure that one day the Darkness would not lay claim to me.

There is so much more to our story, the story of our life together, the boy who stayed and me. I had written that story well before I was brave enough to write this one. It is beautiful. This is not that story. Our story began in this one, but this is about how the Darkness claimed my dad and the shadows began to rest within my mom. She had to survive it, the only way she could. She had to become it when she felt the control of the Darkness over her. She succumbed to the shadowy way of life to keep herself from rocking the boat.

Once she knew she wasn't going to leave, she figured out the only way to stay. The thing she didn't consider was how that would play a leading role in my healing process. I would remember the walks we would take and wonder all the what ifs. What if she had left? Would we have been able to outrun the shadows before they melted into her? Before they followed me and my sister into adulthood? What if we hadn't known about the Darkness at all? What if she could have left the first time she saw him raise a hand to me in anger that one moment, that one day?

The Visit

That particular summer was secretive and long passing. I had been essentially stranded at school with no way to get home unless my parents came to get me. That made the days alone, with little social outlets, terribly painstaking and yet I was also away from the anxiety of home. I had my treasures that I kept close; my walks around campus, the one math class that I ever received an A, sunshine days laying in the grass attempting to enjoy a bit of summer, that weird but quiet room to breathe in, and secret weekend visits from the boy. Those days filled me for the other days. Days like the one where I had a surprise visit from Mom and my sister.

Her shadowy sadness was palpable when I opened the door and my sister looked pale and helpless. She was finally going to leave him. She said, "I can't do it anymore, I'm leaving and taking your sister with me." I was so many things all at once and anxiety welled up in all my internal thoughts.

Not only was I left at a school that without the summer heat and visits from him, felt like a prison, but now she was finally going to leave him. I was going to be left here, and the only thing at home was the Darkness. They were selfish thoughts, but the only thing I knew to do to keep myself from drowning in yet another drama-filled change. One that I had begged and prayed for, years before this day.

I don't remember how long they were there. It felt like another announcement was made and then a leaving. She felt raw, exposed, and drowning in the shadow that she had accepted living with as a companion. How could she go back after deciding to leave, how could she live with herself if she did? I was never sure how the story of that day ended. They came and left as fast as they had arrived.

Fear and hopelessness drove her to see me and I assume a determination to keep quiet and to swallow whatever pride she had left, took her back to him where she stayed. She must have never told him she was coming to see me or that she was planning on leaving him. She would have never gone home if she had.

I went back to my summer days locked away. Somehow as time went by and the Darkness was lessened by miles, it allowed me all the things I needed to keep pushing forward. I went back to the days before that visit. The quiet, the serene, the glowing math grade, the secretive weekends, and the days in the sun with no regrets and no remorse for being a rawer version of me. Home was where Darkness would always reside, but here, I could keep the shadows at bay. For a little while anyway, this new prison had begun to set me free.

Twenty-Four Hours

I managed to float through the next many months, day by day, focusing on the light that kept trying to peek through. I was owned, managed, controlled and ultimately, the relationship with my parents was like breath because I didn't know how to exist without them. 'Don't be with that boy' was a constant and bellowing reminder of their madness and control over me. We had kept our relationship to ourselves that secret summer and now it was time to give it freedom.

I remember Mom coming to pick me up for the weekend one spring day. Things were coming back to life after a snowy cold winter and there was a whispered promise of new in the air that day. I was hoping to have a moment with her at home to explain that the boy and I were together again after our second breakup and it was a forever kind of thing this time. Having to endure a ride home and a night's sleep before that conversation was anxiety-ridden. It wouldn't go well. I knew that, and in the end, it went terribly.

She spoke harshly about the mistakes she knew I was making, her glowing disappointment in me, and she did it all with an overwhelming anger that was becoming more of who she was now. In the end, she told me to gather my things, that she was driving me back to school. No beautiful weekend at home with family, no deep sleeps in my own bed, or cuddles with the Christmas kitty. But, that's not what I had expected, or even hoped for. That's not what home was anyway.

I hadn't unpacked out of anticipation of her actions. I breathed deeply, trying to remind myself that this was not a response to me carving out goodness in my own choices and living my own life. This was all she knew to do to keep herself safe from what would be the course of the Darkness once he knew I was taking control back of my own life. To stay safe from the wrath of Darkness that would come if she didn't play within the shadows and create the chaos herself.

The drive back to school was less than 24 hours from the ride home. I didn't even see my dad. She had me in the car quicker than he was able to put on his robe and flip-flop his way down the stairs. I wasn't sad to have missed that. These were the moments when I could see that the shadows were taking over Mom. The Darkness had penetrated into her now. She had given up resisting it when she decided not to leave and instead of being timid of it and angered by it, she gave in to his way of playing the game.

Trying to, and dreaming about, leaving was not the battle anymore. Her new nightmare was learning to live with it, to behave like it. No more struggling not to drown in it. In order to appease it she was willing to take steps ahead of the Darkness so that we couldn't feel its wrath, only hers. She had chosen to just swallow it up, to become it.

In the days to come, she would somehow make him seem tamed. Essentially, she had created a chaos scenario that was easier for her to handle because it was of her own making. Maybe she thought my sister and I could handle it easier that way too. Maybe she assumed I was a shadow dweller too and I knew she didn't really mean what she said and what she did. Like I could sense her role now and wouldn't feel pain from the Darkness if she covered it first with her own shadow. Maybe she didn't believe any of that and she was just surviving, willing to give up anything else to make sure her pain wouldn't swallow her up. Maybe it was just her own disappointment that I was choosing something that would make the Darkness show itself.

That I wasn't going to feign to his control anymore, scared her more than her own choice to stay in it. I couldn't even be mad at her for it. None of us knew how to make the sun stay up long enough to keep us out of the dark.

I Do, They Don't

From that day until wedding day proved a story all of its own. The Darkness and the Shadow worked as a team now. Things were different, I wasn't protecting her from him anymore. I couldn't trust her with my heart, she was not the Mom who hid away in the shadows with me, she was a stranger who would grant me access to her as a confidant but would collect my transparency as a weapon for the Darkness to use in battle with me.

We were engaged shortly after the quick trip home. I remember the engagement being beautiful and both of them seemingly 'happy' at the time. I was wary of their joy in good things. It was always just enough to create hope and deep breaths. Then the control would come, the threats would be voiced, and hope would fade. It was never a long-lasting happiness, and this was no exception. It is truthfully hurtful to remember it all, and in writing this I am hopeful that seeing it all given life on paper will allow more of that hurt to wash away. At least now, after years of work and deep digging, the tools are there to allow the pain to withdraw without the hurt rooting and taking hold.

I remember so much Darkness during that season of planning, but where it came from, will always be unclear. Was it her or was it him? Was it a team effort, or was it preemptive striking from the Shadow before the Darkness had noticed he was losing his control? I remember Mom standing in her bathroom putting on her makeup. I remember a spring morning, I remember the sun was out and I was about to leave for work as a preschool teacher. I remember a brief conversation about the boy and me and our engagement and the wedding. I remember her mood was shadowed and her face was emotionless. I remember her telling me she didn't care if she ever saw me again.

That was the day I left that house. The once naive White House was now full of new stories of the Dark and the Shadows. I was 20, and out of school. Not because that was ever my plan, but that ended up being the only option at the time for survival. Their many attempts to force me back into their Dark story, played out through my college choices. If you can even call them choices. If I didn't marry this boy and walked away from him forever, I would have the help I needed to finish school, if we chose marriage, I wouldn't.

We chose our marriage. For the boy and I, that was our path and the one we knew we wanted to journey on together. We talked about our choice at length before we made it and we have talked about it many times since. We still wouldn't change our trajectory all those years ago. For the Darkness and the Shadow, that choice meant that they would take their part of school funding away as I wasn't playing by the rules of their games of control and abuse. For me that meant no more hefty school loans to pay, no decisions made for me, and a future with a human who was filled with light and allowed me glimpses of what could be.

School, the way they had designed it, was not proving to be my experience anyway. It was where they placed me, where they sent me away; to control, to undermine, and to keep me in a new kind of entrapment. It had never been about becoming independent and journeying through four years of figuring out who I wanted to be without concern over when I would be taken away or sent back, or shamed into believing I was still a terrible girl who was not meeting standards. It had been a prison of freedoms for one hot summer, and beyond that it was laced with difficulties.

I was willing to let all my original dreams of school and education go to be free of the rest. To begin the long road to healing, I had too. School could have come later on for me, in my own way and my own design and it did in a sense. I claimed my AA Degree years later even though I had taken so many more classes than that would ever give me credit for. I have thought many times about going back and finishing with a new dream. I may still someday, but for now, embracing and grabbing hold of the help I needed, becoming the Mom I had always hoped to be, claiming my story, and owning my own healing has been more of an education than I could have ever paid for.

I had moved home to work and make wedding plans. I left home that dark day because the shadows became overwhelming. I had nowhere to go and somehow leaving felt safer than staying. It wasn't as though I had a choice really. When someone says that they would rather never see you again, you make a new plan. These unpredictable and emotionally abusive attacks left nothing behind but emptiness and now they came from all sides.

At this point, Mom, who in her fear and anger would stay silent for days, had now said terrible things to me, slapped me across the face one dark shadowed morning, and told me that my leaving and never coming back was what she wanted. I could give her that. It seemed that everything I was becoming was a reminder of who she couldn't choose to be. She knew she was losing me and, in a sense, herself too.

I think it became easier for her to live with the Darkness if she was also able to be his codependent and controlled partner. Her movements now were so unlike what I had known before. I couldn't trust either of them to show unmasked kindness, love without control, or allow me to breathe without their restrictive holds. Leaving was terrifying and yet also felt like the day they dropped me at school in that cold room. I was so fearful, but also hopeful for an end of being a part of who they were and who I had to be when I was with them, breathing the same air. I couldn't catch my breath long enough to pause within the hurt of what was happening. I just needed to go.

Once I had left home and was living on my own by the graciousness of wonderful people, the days leading up to the wedding usually involved a phone call from Mom. She wasn't calling to ask to help, or wanting to be a part of creating memories of planning and being excited together. She would call daily instead to remind me of the mistakes I was making, and that I could always back out. She had been hurting. She had been hurting and still breathing in the hurt for a long time. I knew that. She was hurting from an abusive first marriage that she had been brave enough to leave with a young son.

Now, she was so deeply embedded from years into a second one that she had given up on escaping. She had been swallowed up. She was so deeply not the mother I knew, her behavior was erratic, unpredictable and untrustworthy. I knew these things about her and it was always my excuse to give her space no matter how hurtful it was to allow. I was codependent on her and I knew it. I didn't know what that meant then, I only knew it meant that refusing her plea would have made her react even more desperately and I couldn't bear anything more than that daily phone call.

It takes a long time and lots of outside help to know how to set boundaries when you are living in and simply surviving the hard. At that time, all I knew to do was allow it, listen to it, and then spend the rest of the day convincing myself I was okay, that she didn't mean what she was saying or how she was behaving. Her hurt was palpable, transferable, and I didn't have the capacity to hear it and let it go. I was so trapped in wanting, in craving their respect and acknowledgement even after all the abuse and control, that I would pick up the phone every day hoping for a different message.

I was stuck in a reel of insanity expecting different versions of each of them to miraculously emerge. Their marriage was deeply embedded in denials. The shadows that plagued both of them, became the Darkness that tormented me. It wasn't going to be magically different or drastically change to a loving, listening, empathy driven story of a family simply because I wished for it.

At one point, it was made known to me that they were neither one planning on attending the wedding. I was devastated, and also not surprised. How I had designed the ideal wedding day in my head when the actuality needed to be accepted. The push and pull of it all is what made these stories so difficult to live in. It was my dad's sister, who ultimately convinced them they needed to be there. She carried with her much of the same spirit my Grandma had possessed, so of course, he listened. They didn't decide on their own to be at my wedding, they were convinced they needed to be there. It was devastating and also so perfectly them.

In the end, wedding day was a dramatic and literal crazy storm of Mother Earth's timing and the chaos of it all seemed intentional and poetic. We had braved many storms to meet at the altar that day in May and we were symbolically leaving some of them behind while bravely walking towards the conquering of others. Dad walked me down the aisle and I was calm. I was secure and looking towards the face who would lead me into air I could breathe in and lift me up to places I could go without fear. I choose to think of that unanticipated wedding day storm as a reminder of what I had lived in, and with its clearing, a glimpse of what was to come; the hope of refreshment, and a new journey of my own making.

The Darkness within Dad seemed quieter most days now, but I knew that it was because my mom was now superseding any outburst by one of her own. He had a partner who had taken up the shadows and was creating chaos on a stage he had designed. On one magical pre-wedding day, his quietness convinced me that he became that 'polliwog hunting' Dad for a day.

In an emotional moment of trust that I let slip from me, I told him about my dream wedding dress. He saw the wrinkled and folded picture of it I had taken from a magazine and had kept in my purse for months. He teared up, and told me to go buy it along with a veil. He picked out the veil, of course, but he gave me my dream dress. I would wane in my convictions about him that day because of his gift. Just like the gifts of jewels and cards to keep Mom where he needed her. Maybe he had done the same with me now too.

This shifting and waning would happen at times and I would begin to feel like I had made it all up. Like it was just one terribly grim tale that I had maddeningly brought to life. I would allow room for hope. Maybe I really was the one with all the bad in me just like that brown statue that represented me to the Dark all those years ago. Maybe he had rooted that in me or maybe he had simply just made it known for everyone to believe. Maybe it had always been my fault; the arguments, the leaving, the disastrous holidays, the need to buy gifts and cards for a quick fix. I have been living in insanity for so long that maybe I was no longer sane.

These are the things I have always been told after all. After years of the Darkness, these are the things I believed about myself and the words I would recite when I felt I was always the problem. I am pulled into believing that my voice and actions are shameful; my words ridiculous and silenced. I am selfish, I am moody, and those rose-colored glasses keep me too naive to live life without his control. I am messy; a destroyer of relationships in our house, a girl on the prowl, an invitation for boys to be boys. I am a problem; I was meant to be a boy because that is what he had hoped for and mentioned aloud many times.

"He shouldn't have ever been a parent," Mom had said, but he was made one anyway nine short months after their Valentine's Day wedding. I was not allowed to exist without blame, to live without awareness of how strained my emotions were, but I knew that I needed to live a life outside of the shadows. It was a constant gaslighting and I was always on fire.

The wedding dress day was a dream of sorts, but then I learned that they had convinced one another to not be at the wedding at all. To take a stand and make it another day where Shadows came to play in jest. It was a 'tug of war' of a life with our family. Emotionally pulled all the time and in opposite directions was the norm, and it was always unforgiving. At first I had been consumed with the supporting role of holding Mom and my sister, while also clinging to the desire that the Darkness would really see me and accept me because I was his daughter. Now it was a floundering of sorts to hold onto my own life. I was reaching for the light beyond this family and being emotionally ripped apart hoping they would become the version of what I knew other people had always thought we were. We had hidden well in the Dark.

It came much later. The understanding and the truth of how we had lived within an abusive cycle. Emotionally and verbally abused, we had lived in, existed, and breathed in trauma in some way, for so many years. The emotional abuse was secretive, hidden away from people who just knew us on the outside and only suspected by those who knew us well. The physical was so intermittent that it wouldn't even be talked about. That was a chapter within our younger years when it could be accepted and excused without anyone assuming it was wrong.

There were never bruises on the outside. Nothing left that was tangible or questionable. Dad could smile and charm anyone; all those dinners at the Lodge with those servers who felt like family, people we would meet looking at open houses, or his co-pilots who he would meet, and display the pictures of us he kept in his wallet. At home I knew he wished we were boys and Mom wished she hadn't made him a parent. Nobody could see the push and pull, the ebb and flow of the abusive tide, but our insides were ripped wide open. Nobody questioned whether we were okay, they just kept to their own business and assumed we were. Everyone just peered in and believed what they wanted to while I was silently crying out for anyone to see the truth and tell me that none of it had ever been alright.

The day I took myself to counseling after our babies were born was the first day of my new life. Someone looked at me from the inside, beyond the dark of that grief, and told me I was okay. That I was justified in all my feelings. I was finally validated and heard and what I experienced was received without question. I was not to blame for the story I lived. I was told that I was good enough, whole and not broken, and that this was my beginning to healing, finally.

Emotional abuse is devastatingly soul-sucking. The scars run deep and wide and are often reopened in a moment of careless triggering. They can cover the whole inside of a person like the deepest of scar tissue that becomes painfully irritated without warning. They can prompt the seeking of things that are destructive especially when your experience runs through your vulnerable days of youth. I can only tell my own story and hope that the reading of it is as fruitful to your heart healing as it is for me to be writing it.

It is a lifelong pursuit of healing wounds and letting go. You must know that you are golden. You must be aware of your value beyond what any one person can express to you. It might take time for you to know yourself that way. I think I am still processing my own worth forty years beyond those 'polliwog hunting' days in the sun.

The Beginning in the End

The road out of childhood trauma is not a smooth and straight one. It's bumpy, arduous, and full of potholes. It's a road you can never veer off of, not to find continued growth beyond what the child inside you believed about themselves. I will forever be fighting for that little girl. She is resilient. She is incredibly capable of good things. Some days it is easier to believe than others and on those more difficult days, you choose to lead yourself with grace and lots of self-care. The most honest thing to tell yourself is that it was not, in any way fair what you were made to endure. Though you are not a byproduct of what that trauma was, you do contain remnants of it in your own shadows. Those are the shadowed corners that you will work to unveil and release, and when you do, you will see all the beauty and light that hid underneath. It was always there.

In order to be on that daily path of healing, you must revisit the darkness and the shadows to allow the light in. Everyone who has suffered through trauma is on their own unique path and everyone needs time to heal in their own way and their own time. Destructive behavior is not healing, but seeing yourself for what you are beyond that behavior is a great beginning. We all get to have new beginnings and those come every time you celebrate uncovering a dark moment as you're clearing out space for more warmth to cover you.

My story of trauma and abuse is not unlike others in many ways. So many factors are similar in other stories; the shame, the mental anguish, the guilt, the emotional gaslighting, and the irony of needing love, wanting it from those who also keep you captive, while also not seeing yourself as worthy of it. It's devastating that you might have lived in the Darkness just enough to cloud over the goodness that exists outside of it all.

This journal is about what was never noticed because it hid so well in those shadowy corners. I knew it was there. I was reminded any time I started to believe it wasn't. It would recede, but would then shift closer again just like the tide behaves on the shore. It left me captivated and bound by the need to be cared for while also desperately reaching for love that wasn't derived from being good enough or being controlled.

If this was your story too, please know that you were not to blame. None of it was your fault. You were not the cause of the Darkness in your home if you cried out in protection of someone you saw being threatened. The shadows didn't follow you if you spilled your milk at the table. It wasn't your fault that the absence of Light would make him crazed with anger when you were too afraid to jump into the pool. It was all there long before you and it never had the tools to be anything else.

The real tragedy of abuse is not in the moment it begins when you are fighting to see through to another reality. It is not those moments after it has faded into those shadowed corners when the darkness will have you deny it ever took place. Those moments where you agree that it was probably your fault because this person with his darkness were supposed to be your honest protector. It is not in the moments of silent desperation in prayer that it will never happen again. It is not when you continue to love and respect them because that is what you were taught to do. It is not even when the abuse happens again, and again even though you prayed it wouldn't. It always will because there is never just one visit of the Darkness, even if it is left behind by millions of moments without it. The real tragedy isn't that the abuse is a pattern generated by a person with their own deep-rooted pain.

The real tragedy is that once the abusive Darkness has found you and laid its hands on you, it has touched you and the wounds exist now. They are always just on the brink of healing when it happens again building up the scar tissue. It has left you reeling. Reeling from heartless words, chasms of self-doubt and worthlessness that have now begun seeping in and weaving itself through your veins. The real tragedy is that once the abuse is really over, when the 7th attempt to leave means freedom, it also means that the most difficult journey has begun.

You have been so brave, you have fought your way out. You have trudged through the muddy waters because you know the way out now. This is where the tragedy of abuse meets your overwhelming strength. You have the seed of truth within you that says 'you are worth digging out' and now the tearful, dreadful, and heart wrenching work begins. The work of digging deep in order to be able to climb out of the crevices and low laden valleys that the years have backed you into, is tearful and necessary. Your light was never diminished.

The tragedy is that you are the one who has to grow the flame back to what it always was. What it always was to be is now yours to decide. It is time to grieve what you have lived through, and then with everything you have left, dig deep. Your light is waiting to be turned all the way up. The tragedy is that someone has buried your worth, your self-love, your self-respect, and your bright light and now YOU have to fight to uncover it. You will have to fight to live a life away from those chasms and valleys that held you captive for so long. The real tragedy is when you work so hard to dig and climb your way out, the first time won't be the last time you have to. The healing of abuse is long term, disciplined and intentional. You have to be the hero of your healing story.

I am so sorry. I am sorry that you were hurt so deeply and for so long. I am sorry that the younger version of you might be stuck there. I am sorry that you have to work so hard to help them heal. I am sorry that your journey to your healing is frightening and I am sorry that it is also essential. You are worth the digging and the climbing. You have always been worth the journey. You are worth the hardest of days, the brilliantly light filled ones, and all that fall in the in-between. You are a beautiful being and the Light is ready for you.

I hope that when you're out of the despair of it and those darker memories come fewer and farther between, you can look back on some of what you lived through and breathe into what you knew was good. To breathe into your own version of those 'polliwog hunting days'. Those moments were the ones that gave your light just enough air to keep a small flame within for you to find and reclaim again.

In many ways, I will always be seeking those polliwog hunting days. I often wonder if my dad is too. We don't talk about these flashes of memory together nor do we discuss his Darkness. Not anymore. We did once, for me, when I first knew that I needed to ask him about all of it. It was difficult and as I assumed he would, he denied most of the memories that I wrote about, but then again, he always took himself out of the madness he created. To hope for different when he hasn't uncovered his own story is insanity on my part: a disruption and a set back to my own journey.

He remembers the polliwogs though. He remembers the Sunday drives, afternoons at Grandma's, and the open houses too. He loves to relive the bike rides, the nights by the fire and looking at the stars. He loves the wedding dress story, since he played the role of hero, of course, and still spends hours looking at greeting cards for Mom and sometimes for us too. I know he is wounded and I know his shadowed corners are deeply rooted in that boy. That boy that still lives in his darkest of corners looking for a way into the warmth and the treats and the love.

My healing allows me to see him through different lenses most days. I only enjoy what he is able to give and don't allow myself to grieve what I know he cannot. I have to let the rest of the hope in what could have been go. All that hope is placed in me now, all the goodness and the light is placed in my own family instead. I have broken the cycle of trauma and it has been the legacy and work of my life.

Now, he is simply the dad I remember on those chilly northern California mornings when we would search for those polliwogs. I think I loved those little champions of growth and change because I could watch it all happen. Each day was a new transition into a new version of themselves. Each day brought a new part of them to the surface that would eventually turn them into what they were always meant to be. They started out one way, and ended up another before we took them back home to live their life and they did it all themselves. The growth was visible and the change was miraculous.

I couldn't have known then, how big, and dark, and brutal, the story of my own evolving would be for me, but I am so glad I embraced it and found my way to being released from the dark that kept me a prisoner. I wish Dad would have allowed his own evolutionary freedom too. His Darkness has seemed to fade with age, denial, and time, but I know that boy who was left out in the cold is still waiting for his freedom from the dark.

I have chosen to separate myself from so much, many years ago, that the knowledge of the why and how of the puzzle pieces is not something I desire anymore. Most days, I am left giving grace to that boy left out in the cold. It is the only gift I have to give and one he will never know I have given.

Above all, I am grateful for the story that has come from the Dark so that I can share it with you. I keep a daily promise to my healing and I hope that you can do the same. I am so glad you are here. The puzzle pieces are laid out, ready and waiting. The light is calling.